THE SEVEN CAPITAL SINS

The Seven Capital Sins

FULTON J. SHEEN, PhD, DD

*Agrégé en Philosophie de L'Université de Louvain and
The Catholic University of America*

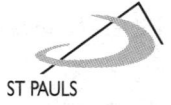

ST PAULS

Library of Congress Cataloging-in-Publication Data

Sheen, Fulton J. (Fulton John), 1895-1979.
 The seven capital sins / Fulton J. Sheen.
  p. cm.
 Originally published by Our Sunday Visitor, Huntington, Indiana
 ISBN 0-8189-0891-2 (alk. paper)
 1. Deadly sins. 2. Spiritual life—Catholic Church. 3. Jesus
Christ— Crucifixion. I. Title.

 BV4626.S465 2000
 241'.3 — dc21

                                                    00-048499

Imprimatur:
John Francis Noll, DD
Bishop of Fort Wayne

ISBN 10: 0-8189-0891-2
ISBN 13: 978-0-8189-0891-0

Eight addresses delivered in the nationwide Catholic Hour, produced by
the National Council of Catholic Men, in cooperation with the National
Broadcasting Company on Sundays from February 26 to April 9, 1939
and on Good Friday April 7, 1939.

This Alba House edition is produced by special arrangement
with the Estate of Fulton J. Sheen and the Society for the
Propagation of the Faith, 366 Fifth Avenue, New York, NY 10001. It
has been revised to incorporate a more recent and more recognizable
translation of the Scripture texts.

This book is published in the United States of America
by Alba House, the publishing arm of the Society of St. Paul,
an international religious congregation of priests and brothers
serving the Church through the communications media.

Printing Information:

Current Printing - first digit   5 6 7 8 9 10

Year of Current Printing - first year shown

          2014 2015 2016 2017 2018 2019 2020

TO MARY IMMACULATE
with filial homage

A special word of thanks to
Fr. Jim Sullivan, OMI
Our Lady of Lourdes Parish
Lesmurdie, Western Australia

and the

Fulton J. Sheen Society of Perth Western Australia, Inc.
for having encouraged the publication of this book
and provided us with the text of this fine work.

TABLE OF CONTENTS

THE SEVEN CAPITAL SINS

I

THE FIRST WORD: ANGER

"Father, forgive them, for they know not what they do."

The First Word from the Cross was in reparation for the sin of anger. The one passion in man which has deeper roots in his rational nature than any other, is the passion of anger. Anger and reason are capable of great compatibility, because anger is based upon reason which weighs both the injury done and the satisfaction to be demanded. We are never angry unless someone has injured us in some way—or we think he has.

But not all anger is sinful, for there is such a thing as just anger. The most perfect expression of just anger we find in Our Blessed Lord cleansing the Temple. Passing through its shadowed doorways at the festival of the Pasch, He found greedy traders, victimizing at every turn the worshipers who needed lambs and doves for the Temple sacrifices. Making a scourge of little cords He moved through their midst with a calm dignity and beautiful self-control even more compelling than the whip. The oxen and sheep He drove out with His scourge; with His hands He upset the tables of the money changers who scrambled on the floor after their rolling coins; with His finger He pointed to the venders of doves as He bade them leave the outer court; to all He said: "Get these things out of here, and do not make My Father's house a market place." Here was fulfilled the injunction of the Scriptures, "Be angry, and sin not"; for anger is no sin under three conditions: (1) If the cause of the anger be just, for example, defense of God's honor; (2) If it be no greater than the cause demands, that is, if it be kept under control; and (3) If it be quickly subdued: "Let not the sun go down upon your anger."

Here we are not concerned with just anger, but with unjust anger, namely, that which has no rightful cause—anger which is excessive, revengeful, and enduring; the kind of anger and hatred against God which has destroyed religion on one-sixth of the earth's surface and which has burned countless churches and chapels and murdered more servants of God than in any other century prior to our own; the kind of hatred which is not only directed against God, but also against fellowmen, and is fanned by the disciples of class conflict who talk peace but glory in war; the red anger which rushes the blood to the surface, and the white anger which pushes it to the depths and bleaches the face; the anger which seeks to "get even," to repay in kind, bump for bump, punch for punch, eye for eye, lie for lie; the anger of the clenched fist prepared to strike not in defense of that which is loved but in offense against that which is hated; the kind of anger which will destroy our civilization unless it is smothered by love.

Our Blessed Lord came to make reparation for the sin of anger, first by teaching us a prayer: "Forgive us our trespasses as we forgive those who trespass against us"; and then by giving us a precept: "Love your enemies, do good to those who hate you." More concretely still, He added: "If anyone forces you to go one mile, go with him for two.... If anyone wants to... take your tunic, give him your cloak as well." Revenge and retaliation were forbidden: "You have heard that it was said: An eye for an eye, and a tooth for a tooth.... But I tell you, Love your enemies." These precepts were made all the more striking because He practiced them. When the Gerasenes became angry at Him because He put a higher value on an afflicted man than on a herd of swine, Scripture records no retort: "And getting into the boat, He crossed over the water and came to His own town." To the soldier who struck Him with a mailed fist, He meekly responded: "If I have spoken wrongly, bear witness against the wrong; but if I have spoken rightly, why do you hit Me?"

The perfect reparation for anger was made on Calvary. We might almost say that anger and hate led Him up that hill. His own people hated Him for they asked for His crucifixion; the law hated Him for it forsook justice to condemn Justice; the Gentiles hated Him, for they consented to His death; the forests hated Him for one of its trees bore the burden of His weight; the flowers hated Him as they wove thorns for His brow; the bowels of the earth hated Him as it gave its steel as hammer and nails. Then, as if to personalize all that hatred, the first generation of clenched fists in the history of the world stood beneath the Cross and shook them in the face of God. That day they tore His body to shreds as in this day they smash His tabernacle to bits. Their sons and daughters smash crucifixes as they once smote the Crucified on Calvary. Let no one think the clenched fist is a phenomenon of our present century; they whose hearts freeze into fists today are but the successors of those who stood beneath a Cross with hands lifted like clubs against Love two thousand years ago.

As one contemplates those clenched fists, one cannot help but feel that if ever anger would have been justified, if ever Justice might have fittingly judged, if ever Power might have rightfully struck, if ever Innocence might have lawfully protested, if ever God might have lawfully revenged Himself against man—it was at this moment. And yet just at that second when a sickle and a hammer combined to cut down the grass on Calvary's hill, erect a cross and drive nails through Hands to render impotent the blessings of Love Incarnate, He, like a tree which bathes in perfume the axe which kills it, lets fall from His lips for the earth's first hearing the perfect reparation for anger and hate—a prayer for the army of clenched fists, the First Word from the Cross: "Father, forgive them, for they know not what they do."

The greatest sinner may now be saved; the blackest sin may now be blotted out; the clenched fist may now be opened; the unforgivable may now be forgiven. While they were most certain they knew what they were doing, He seizes upon the only possible palliation of their crime, and urges it upon His Heavenly Father with all the ardor of a merciful Heart: *ignorance*—"They know not what they do." If they did know what they were doing as they fastened Love to a tree, and still went on doing it, they would never be saved. They would be *damned*. It was only because fists are clenched in ignorance that they may yet be opened into folded hands; it is only because tongues blaspheme in ignorance that they may yet speak in prayer. It is not their conscious wisdom that saves them; it is their unconscious ignorance.

The word from the Cross teaches us two lessons: (1) The reason for forgiving is ignorance; and (2) There are no limits to forgiveness.

The reason for forgiveness is ignorance. Divine

Innocence found such a reason for pardon; certainly guilt can do no less. St. Peter's first Pentecostal sermons used this very excuse of ignorance for the Crucifixion so fresh in his mind: "You killed the author of life, whom God then raised from the dead…. And now, brothers, I know that you acted out of ignorance, as did your rulers." If there were full consciousness of the evil, perfect deliberation, perfect understanding of the consequences of acts, there would be no room for forgiveness. That is why there is no redemption for the fallen angels. They knew what they were doing. We do not. We are very ignorant—ignorant of ourselves and ignorant of others.

Ignorant of others! How little we know of their motives, their good faith, the circumstances surrounding their actions. When others visit violence upon us, we too often forget how little we know about their hearts and say: "I cannot see that there is the slightest excuse; they knew very well what they were doing." And yet in exactly the same circumstances, Jesus found an excuse: "They know not what they do." We know nothing about the inside of our neighbor's heart and hence we refuse to forgive; He knew the heart inside out and because He did know, He forgave. Take any accident scene, let five people look upon it, and you get five different stories about what happened. No one of them sees all sides. Our Lord does and that is why He forgives.

Why is it that we can find excuses for our anger against our neighbor, and yet we refuse to admit the same excuses when our neighbor is angry with us? We say others would forgive us if they understood us perfectly, and that the only reason they are angry with us is because "they do not understand." Why is not that ignorance reversible? Can we not be as ignorant of their motives, as we say they are ignorant of ours? Does not our refusal to find an excuse for their hatred tacitly mean that under similar circumstances we ourselves will be unfit to be forgiven?

Catholics then must not hate the bigots, the Communists, and the persecutors of the Church, for most of them know not what they do. To all who write me venomous letters about the Church I answer: "I quite understand your hatred of the Church and its priesthood. If I had your education, had been told exactly the same untruths about it that you have been told, and believed all the libels spoken against it that you believe, with my own peculiar character and disposition I would hate the Church ten times more than you do. You really do not hate the Catholic Church, you hate only what you believe about the Church." We cannot claim our share in the forgiveness of the First Word from the Cross, unless we are ready to make excuses for others, as Our Lord made them for us. We pray to be forgiven our trespasses, but such forgiveness will be extended only on one condition, and not otherwise, and that is "as we forgive those who trespass against us."

Ignorance of ourselves is another reason for forgiving others. Unfortunately it is ourselves we know least; our neighbor's sins, weaknesses, and failures we know a thousand times better than our own. Criticism of others may be bad, but it is want of self-criticism which is worse. It would be less wrong to criticize others if we first criticized ourselves, for if we first turned the searchlight into our own souls, we would never feel we had a right to turn it on the soul of anyone else. It is only because we are ignorant of our true condition that we fail to realize how badly we stand in need of pardon. Have we ever offended God? Has He any right to be angry with us? Then why should we who need pardon so badly strive not to purchase it by pardoning others? The answer is because we never examine our own consciences. We are so ignorant of our true condition that we know little more of ourselves than our name and address and how much we have—of our selfishness, our envy, our detraction, our sin, we know absolutely nothing. In fact, in order that we may never know ourselves we hate silence and solitariness. Lest our conscience should carry on with us an unbearable repartee we drown out its voice in amusements, distraction, and noise. If we met ourselves in others, we would hate them. If we knew ourselves better, we would be more forgiving of others. The harder we are on ourselves, the easier we will be on others; the man who has never learned to obey knows not how to command; and the man who has never disciplined himself knows not how to be merciful. It is always the selfish who are unkind to others, and those who are hardest on themselves are the kindest to others, as the teacher who knows the least is always the most intolerant of his pupils.

Only a Lord Who thought so little of Himself as to become man and die like a criminal could ever forgive the weakness of those who crucified Him. It is not hatred that is wrong; it is hating the wrong thing that is wrong. It is not anger that is wrong, it is being angry at the wrong thing that is wrong. Tell me your enemy and I will tell you what you are. Tell me your hatred and I will tell you your character. Do you hate religion? Then your conscience bothers you. Do you hate capitalists? Then you are avaricious and you want to be a capitalist. Do you hate the laborer? Then you are selfish and a snob. Do you hate sin? Then you love God. Do you hate your hate, your selfishness, your quick temper, your wickedness? Then you are a good soul, for "If anyone comes to me… and does not hate his own life, he cannot be my disciple."

The second lesson to be derived from this First Word from the Cross is that there is no limit to pardon. Our Lord forgave when He was innocent and not because He Himself had been forgiven.

Hence we must forgive not only when we have been forgiven, but even when we are innocent. The problem of the limits of pardon once troubled Peter and he asked Our Lord: "Lord, how many times can my brother offend me, and I forgive him? Up to seven times?" Peter thought he was stretching forgiveness by saying seven times, for it was four more than the Jewish Masters enjoined. Peter proposed a limit beyond which there was to be no forgiveness. Peter assumed the right to be forgiven is automatically renounced after seven offenses. It is equivalent to saying: "I renounce my right to collect debts from you if you never owe me more than seven dollars, but if you exceed that sum, then my duty of further cancellation ceases. I can throttle you for eight dollars."

Our Lord in answering Peter says forgiveness has no limits: forgiveness is the surrender of all rights and the denial of limits. "I do not say to you, up to seven times; but up to seventy times seven times." That does not mean four hundred ninety, but infinity. The Savior then proceeded to tell the parable of the unjust steward who immediately after being forgiven by his lord a debt of ten thousand talents, choked a fellow servant who owed him a hundred pence. The clear implication is that the offenses for which God forgives us are out of all proportion to the offenses our neighbors commit against us; the proportion mentioned in the parable being one and a quarter million to one. The unmerciful steward by refusing to be merciful to his debtor had his own mercy revoked. His guilt was not that, needing mercy, he refused to show it, but having received mercy, he was unmerciful still. "That is what My heavenly Father will do to you, unless each of you forgives your brother from your heart."

Forgive then and we will be forgiven; remit our anger against others and God will remit His anger against us. Judgment is a harvest where we sow what we reap. If we sowed anger against our brethren during life, we will reap the just anger of God. Judge not and we shall not be judged. If during life we forgive others from our hearts, on Judgment Day the All Wise God will permit something very unusual to Himself: He will forget how to add and will know only how to subtract. He Who has a Memory from all eternity will no longer remember our sins. Thus we will be saved once again through Divine "Ignorance." By forgiving others on the ground that they know not what they do, Our Lord will forgive us on the ground that He no longer remembers what we did. It may well be that if He looks on a hand that, now after hearing the First Word on the Cross, gives a kindly blessing to an enemy, He will even forget that it was once a clenched fist red with the blood of Christendom.

And dars't thou venture still to live in sin,
And crucify thy dying Lord again?
Were not his pangs sufficient? Must he bleed
Yet more? O, must our sinful pleasures feed
Upon his torments, and augment the story
Of the sad passion of the Lord of glory!
Is there no pity? Is there no remorse
In human breasts? Is there a firm divorce
Betwixt all mercy and the hearts of men?
Parted for ever,—ne'er to meet again?
No mercy bides with us: 'tis thou alone,
Hast it, sweet Jesu, for us, that have none
For thee; thou hast forestall'd our markets so,
That all's above, and we have none below:
Nay, blessed Lord, we have not wherewithal
To serve our shiftless selves: unless we call
To thee, thou art our Saviour, and hast power
To give, and whom we crucify each hour:
We are cruel, Lord, to thee, and ourselves too;
Jesu forgive us; we know not what we do.

(Francis Quarles)

II

THE SECOND WORD: ENVY

"This day you shall be with Me in Paradise."

The Second Word from the Cross was in reparation for the sin of envy. Envy is sadness at another's good and joy at another's evil. What rust is to iron, what moths are to wool, what termites are to wood, that envy is to the soul: the assassination of brotherly love. We are not here concerned with just envy or zeal which inspires us to emulate good example and to progress with those who are our betters, for the Scriptures enjoin us to "be zealous for spiritual gifts"; rather we here touch on that sinful envy which is a wilful grieving at another's good, either spiritual or temporal, for the reason that it seems to diminish our own good. The honor paid to another is regarded by the envious man as a reflected disgrace on himself and he is sad in consequence. Envy manifests itself in discord, hatred, malicious joy, backbiting, detraction, imputing of evil motives, jealousy, and calumny. A sample of this kind of envy we find in one of the two women who asked Solomon to adjudicate their dispute. The first woman said: "This woman and I live in the same house…. This woman's child died during the night, for in her sleep she smothered him by lying on him. Later that night she got up and took my child from my side, as I, your handmaid was sleeping… and laid her dead child in my bosom." To which the other woman answered: "That is not so! The dead child is yours, the living child is mine."

Since there were no witnesses, Solomon ordered a sword to be brought to him, for he rightly judged that the motherly heart of the real mother would rather give up her child than see it killed. Brandishing the glittering sword he said: "Divide the living child in two, and give half to the one, and half to the other." Hearing this the woman whose child was alive cried out in terror and pity: "I beseech you, my lord, give her the child alive, and do not kill it." But the other said: "Let it be neither mine nor yours; divide it." Then the king commanded the child be given to her who would rather give it up to another than have it killed, knowing that she must be the mother. The point of the story is that envy which is so jealous of the good of another may reach a point where it scruples not to take a life.

In our times, envy has taken on an economic

form. The avarice of the rich is being matched by the envy of the poor. Some poor hate the rich not because they have unjustly stolen their possessions, but because *they* want their possessions. Certain *have-nots* are scandalized at the wealth of the *haves,* only because they are tempted by lust for their possessions. The poor often hate the rich only because they want to be rich themselves; they envy the rich not so much because of their need, but because of their greed. Combined with this is social envy or snobbery which sneers at the higher position of others, because the snobs want to sit in their chairs and enjoy their applause. They assume that in not arriving at such popular favor themselves they were deprived of their due. That is why we hate those who do not pay sufficient attention to us and why we love those who flatter us. If envy is on the increase today, as it undoubtedly is, it is because of the surrender of the belief of a future life and righteous Divine Justice. If this life is all, they think they should have all. From that point on, envy of others becomes their rule of life.

Our Lord was unceasing in His preaching against envy. To those who were envious of the mercy extended the lost sheep He pictured the angels of heaven rejoicing more at the one sinner doing penance than at the ninety-nine just who did not need to do penance. To those who were envious of wealth He warned: "Do not store up treasures for yourselves on earth, where moth and rust destroy, and where thieves break in and steal. Rather store up treasures for yourselves in heaven, where neither moth nor rust destroy, and where thieves neither break in nor steal." To those who were envious of power, such as the Apostles quarreling about who was to be first in the Kingdom, He placed a little child in their midst and putting His arms around him reminded them that heaven was open only to those who were as simple children, for Christ is not in the great but in the small: "Whoever receives one such child in My name, receives Me. And whoever receives Me, receives not Me, but the One Who sent Me."

But His preaching against envy did not save Him from the envious. Pilate was envious of His power; Annas was envious of His innocence; Caiaphas was envious of His popularity; Herod was envious of His moral superiority; the Scribes and Pharisees were envious of His wisdom. Each of these had built his judgment seat of mock moral superiority from which to sentence Morality to the Cross. And in order that He might no longer be a person to be envied they reputed Him with the wicked. Born between an ox and an ass, they now crucify Him between two criminals. That was the last insult they could give Him. To the public eye they created the impression that three thieves and not two were silhouetted against the sky. In a certain sense it was true: two stole gold out of avarice, one stole hearts out of love. *Salvandus, Salvator,* and *Salvatus*: The thief who could have been saved; the thief who was saved; and the Savior who saved them. The crosses spelled out the words Envy, Mercy, and Pity.

The thief on the left envied the Power which Our Blessed Lord claimed. As the chief priests, scribes, and ancients ridiculed the Savior, sneering: "He saved others—himself he cannot save," the thief on the left added to their revilings: "Aren't you the Messiah? Then save yourself and us." In other words: 'If I had that power of yours, that power which you claim as the Messiah, I would use it differently than to hang helpless on a tree. I would step down from the Cross, smite my enemies, and prove what power really is.' Thus did Envy reveal that if it had the gifts which it envies in others it would misuse them, as the thief on the left would have surrendered redemption from sin for release from a nail. In like manner many in the world today who are envious of wealth would probably lose their souls if they had that wealth. Envy never thinks of responsibilities. Looking only to self it misuses every gift that comes its way.

Pity has quite a different effect on the soul. The thief on the right had no envy of the Master's Power but only pity for the Master's sufferings. Rebuking his companion on the left, the good thief said: "Have you no fear of God, seeing that you are under the same sentence? And we indeed, justly, for we're being paid back fittingly for what we did; but this man has done nothing wrong." There was not a spark of envy in him. He wanted nothing in all the world, not even to be removed from tragic companioning with his cross. He was not envious of God's Power, for God knows best what to do with His Power. He was not envious of his fellowmen, for they had nothing worth giving. So he threw himself upon Divine Providence and asked only for forgiveness: "Lord, remember me when You come into Your Kingdom." A dying man asked a dying Man for life; a man without possessions asked a Poor Man for a Kingdom; a thief at the door of death asked to die a thief and steal Paradise. And because he envied nothing, he received all: "Amen, I say to you, this day you shall be with Me in Paradise." One would have thought a saint would have been the first soul purchased over the counter of Calvary by the red coins of redemption, but in the Divine plan it is a thief who steals that privilege and marches as the escort of the King of Kings into Paradise.

Two lessons are taught us by this Second Word from the Cross. The first is that envy is the source of our wrong judgments about others. The chances are that if we are envious of others, nine times out of ten we will misjudge their characters. Because the thief on the left was envious of the Power of Our Lord, he misjudged Him and missed both the

Divinity of the Savior and his own salvation. He falsely argued that Power should always be used the way he would have used it, namely to turn nails into rosebuds, a cross into a throne, blood into royal purple, and the blades of grass on the hillside into bayonets of offensive steel. No one in the history of the world ever came closer to Redemption, and yet no one ever missed it so far. His envy made him ask for the wrong thing: he asked to be taken down when he should have asked to be taken up. It makes one think of how much the envy of Herod resulted in an equally false judgment: He massacred the Innocents because he thought the Infant King came to destroy an earthly kingdom, whereas He came only to announce a heavenly one.

So it is with us. Backbiting, calumny, false judgments, are all born of our envy. We say: "Oh, he is jealous," or "she is jealous"; but how do we know that he or she is jealous unless we ourselves have felt that way? How do we know others are acting proudly unless we know how pride asserts itself? Every envious word is based on a false judgment of our own moral superiority. To sit in judgment makes us feel that we are above those who are judged and more righteous and more innocent than they. To accuse others is to say: "I am not like that." To be envious of others, is to say: "You have stolen that which is mine." Envy of others' wealth has resulted in the gross misjudgment that the best way to do away with its abuse in the hands of the rich is to dispossess them violently, so that the dispossessors may in their turn enjoy its abuse. Envy of others' political power has given rise to the erroneous philosophy that even governments may be overthrown if organized violence is strong enough to do so. Envy thus becomes the denial of all justice and love. In individuals it develops a cynicism which destroys all moral values, for by bankrupting others do we ourselves become bankrupt. In groups it produces a deceit which extends the glad hand of welcome to those who differ, only until they are strong enough to cut it off.

Since envy is so rampant in the world today, it is extremely good counsel to disbelieve 99 per cent of the wicked statements we hear about others. Think of how much the thief on the right had to discount in order to arrive at the truth. He had to disbelieve the judgment of four envious judges, the raillery of envious scribes and ancients, the blasphemous utterances of curious onlookers who love murders, and the envious taunts of the thief on the left who was willing to lose his soul if only he could keep his fingers nimble for more thefts. But if he had been envious of the Lord's Power, he would never have been saved. He found peace by disbelieving the envious scandal mongers. Our peace is found in the same incredulity. The chances are that there is a bit of jealousy, a bit of envy, behind every cutting remark and barbed whispering we hear about our neighbor. It is well to remember that there are always more sticks under the tree that has the most apples. It should be some consolation for those who are so unjustly attacked to remember that it is a physical impossibility for any man to get ahead of us who stays behind to kick us.

A second lesson to be learned from this Word is that the only way to overcome envy is, like the thief on the right, to show pity. As Christians in good faith we are all members of the Mystical Body of Christ, and should therefore love one another as Christ has loved us. If our arm suffers an injury our whole body feels the pain. In like manner, if the Church in any part of the world suffers martyrdom we should feel pity toward it as part of our body, and that pity should express itself in prayer and good works. Pity should be extended not only to those outside the Church who are living as if the earth never bore a Cross, but even to the enemies of the Church who would destroy even the shadow of the Cross. God is their Judge; not we. And as potential brothers of Christ, sons of a Heavenly Father and children of Mary, they must be worth our pity since they were worth the Savior's blood. Unfortunately, there are some who blame the Church for receiving great sinners into the Church on their deathbeds. A few years ago one who was generally believed to be a racketeer and murderer met death at the hands of his fellow criminals. A few minutes before his death, he asked to be received into the Church, was baptized, received First Communion, was anointed and given the last blessing. Some who should have known better protested against the Church. Imagine! Envy at the salvation of a soul! Why not rather rejoice in God's Mercy, for after all did he not belong to the same profession as the thief on the right—and why should not Our Lord be just as anxious to save twentieth century thieves as first century thieves? They both have souls. It would seem that sinful envy of the salvation of a thief is a greater sin than thievery.

One thief was saved: therefore let no one despair. One thief was lost: therefore let no one presume. Have pity then on the miserable and Divine Mercy will be the reward for your pity. When the Pharisees accused Our Lord of eating with publicans and sinners He retorted by reiterating the necessity of mercy: "The healthy do not need a doctor, but sick persons do. Now go and learn what this means; *I desire mercy and not sacrifice.* For I came not to call the righteous, but sinners."

One day a woman went to the saintly Father John Vianney, the Curé of Ars, in France, and said: "My husband has not been to the sacraments or to Mass for years. He has been unfaithful, wicked, and unjust. He has just fallen from a bridge and was drowned—a double death of body and soul." The

Curé answered: "Madam, there is a short distance between the bridge and the water, and it is that distance which forbids you to judge." There was just that distance between the two crosses which saved the penitent thief. If the thief on the right had been self-righteous, he would have looked down on Jesus and lost his soul. But because he was conscious of his own sin, he left room for Divine Pardon. And the answer of the Redeemer to his request proves that to the merciful, love is blind—for if we love God and our neighbor, who may even be our enemy, Divine Love will go blind as it did for the thief on the right. Christ will no longer be able to see our faults, and that blindness will be for us the dawn of the vision of Love.

> "Say, bold but blessed thief,
> That in a trice
> Slipped into paradise,
> And in plain day
> Stol'st heaven away,
> What trick couldst' thou invent
> To compass thy intent?
> What arms?
> What charms?"
> "Love and belief."
>
> "Say, bold but blessed thief,
> How couldst thou read
> A crown upon that head?
> What text, what gloss—

A kingdom and a cross?
How couldst thou come to spy
God in a man to die?
What light?
What sight?"
"The sight of grief—

"I sight to God his pain;
And by that sight
I saw the light,
Thus did my grief
Beget relief.
And take this rule from me,
Pity thou him he'll pity thee.
Use this,
Ne'er miss,
Heaven may be stolen again."

(Anonymous)

III

THE THIRD WORD: LUST

"Woman, behold your son… son, behold your mother."

The Third Word from the Cross was in reparation for the sin of lust. Lust is an inordinate love of the pleasures of the flesh. The important word here is *inordinate* for it was Almighty God Himself who associated pleasure with the flesh. He attached pleasure to eating in order that we might not be remiss in nourishing and preserving our individual lives; He associated pleasure with the marital act in order that husband and wife might not be remiss in their social obligations to propagate humankind and raise children for the Kingdom of God. The pleasure becomes sinful at that point where, instead of using it as means, we begin to use it as an end. To eat for the sake of eating is a sin, because eating is a means to an end, which is health. Lust, in like manner, is selfishness or perverted love. It looks not so much to the good of the other, as to the pleasure of self. It breaks the glass that holds the wine; it breaks the lute to snare the music. It subordinates the other to self for the sake of pleasure. Denying the quality of "otherness" it seeks to make the other person care for us, but not to make us care for the other person.

We are living today in what might properly be called an era of carnality. As the appeal to the spiritual relaxes, the demands of the flesh increase. Living less for God, human nature begins to live only for self, for "no one can serve two masters: either he will hate the one, and love the other; or he will sustain the one, and despise the other." Peculiar to this era of carnality is the tendency to equate the perpetuity of marriage with the fleshly pleasure, so that when the pleasure ends the bond is presumed to be automatically dissolved. In America, for example, there is one divorce for every four marriages—an indication of how much we have ceased to be a Christian nation and how much we have forgotten the words of Our Lord: "What God has joined together, let no one separate." The regrettable aspect of it all is that with this increased sin there is a decreased sense of sin. Souls sin more, but think less about it. Like the sick who are so moribund they have no desire to be better, sinners become so calloused they have no yearning for redemption. Having lost their eyes, they no longer want to see; the only pleasure left them in the end is to mock and sneer at those who do. It is never the pure who say chastity is impossible, but only the impure. We judge others by ourselves, and attribute to others the vices from which we ourselves refuse to abstain.

Some reparation had to be made for the sin of lust which in Old Testament times became so hideous to God that He would have withheld the destruction of the cities of Sodom and Gomorrah could but ten just men have been found within their gates. Our Lord began making reparation for it at the first moment of the Incarnation for He chose to be born of a virgin. Why did He choose to transcend the laws of nature? The answer is very simple. Original sin has been propagated to every human being, with the exception of Our Lady, from Adam to this very hour. The prolongation of this taint in human nature takes place through the carnal act, of which man is the active principle, for man was the head of the human race. Every time there is generation of one human being by another, through the union of man and woman, there is the propagation of original sin.

The problem confronting the Second Person of the Blessed Trinity in becoming man was: How become man without at the same time becoming sinful man, that is, man infected by the sin to which all flesh is heir? How become man without inheriting original sin? He had to be a true man in order to suffer for man, but He could not be a sinful man if He were to redeem man from sin. How could He be both man and yet sinless? He could be man by being born of a woman; He could be sinless man, without original sin, by dispensing with man as the active principle of generation—in other words, by being born of a virgin. Thus it was that when the Angel Gabriel appeared to Mary and told her that she was to conceive the Messiah whose name would be called Jesus, she answered: "How will this come about, since I do not know man?" She had the vow of virginity and she intended to keep it. The Angel answered that the conception of the Son of Man would take place without man, through the power of the Holy Spirit who would overshadow her. Being assured of her continued virginity, she accepted the motherhood of God Incarnate. "Let it be done to me according to your word." So it was that the reparation for sins of the flesh began the first moment of the Incarnation through the Virgin Birth. That same love He manifested for virginity in the beginning, He re-echoed in the first sermon of His public life: "Blessed are the pure of heart, for they shall see God." Later on, to the Scribes and Pharisees who sought to malign His good name, He challenged them to find anything impure in His life. "Which of you can convict Me of sin?"

The final atonement and reparation is made on Calvary where, in reparation for all the impure desires and thoughts of men, Our Lord is crowned with thorns; where, in reparation for all the sins of shame, He is stripped of His garments; where, in reparation for all the lusts of the flesh, He is almost dispossessed of His flesh, for according to Sacred Scripture the very bones of His Body could be numbered. We are so used to looking upon artistic crucifixes of ivory and the beautiful images in our prayer books, that we think of Our Blessed Lord as being whole on the Cross. The fact is that He made such reparation for sins of the flesh that His Body was torn, His blood poured forth, and Scripture refers to Him on the Cross as a leper, as one struck by God and afflicted, so that "there was in him no stately bearing to make us look at him, nor appearance that would attract us to him."

Our Lord chose to go even further in reparation for the sins of lust by dispossessing Himself of the two most legitimate claims of the flesh. If there was ever a pure and legitimate claim in the realm of the flesh, it is the claim to the love of one's own Mother. If there is any honest title to affection in the universe of the flesh, it is the bonds of love which attach us to another human being. But the flesh was so misused by man and so perverted that Our Divine Savior renounced even these legitimate bonds of the flesh in order to atone for the illegitimate. He became totally un-fleshed, in order to atone for the abuse of the flesh, by giving away His Mother and His best friend. So to His own Mother He looks and bids farewell: "Woman, behold your son"; and to

His best friend He looks and bids farewell again: "Behold your mother."

How different from the world. A mother will deprive her son of an advanced education in a foreign land, saying: "I cannot give up my son"; or a wife will deprive her husband of good material advancement through a short absence, saying: "I cannot give up my husband." These are not the cries of noble love but of attachment. Our Lord did not say: "I cannot give up My Mother." He gave her up. He loved her enough to give her away for her life's plan and destiny, namely, to be *our* Mother. Here was a love that was strong enough to forget itself, in order that others might never want for love. He made the sacrifice of His Mother that we might have her; He wounded Himself like the pelican, that we might be nourished by her motherhood. Mary accepted the poor exchange to carry out her Son's redemptive work. And at that moment when Jesus surrendered even the legitimate claims of the flesh and gave us His Mother, Mary, and His best friend, John—selfishness died its death.

Two lessons are to be learned from this Third Word from the Cross: (1) The only real escape from the demands of the flesh is to find something more than the flesh to love; and (2) Mary is the refuge of sinners.

If we could ever find anything we loved more than the flesh, the demands of the flesh would be less imperative. This is the "escape" a mother offers her boy when she says: "Don't do anything of which your mother would ever be ashamed." If there is that higher love of his mother, the boy will always have a consecrated sense of affection, something for which he will be willing to make sacrifices. When a mother makes such an appeal to her son she is merely re-echoing the lesson of the Savior, Who, in giving His Mother to us as our Mother, equivalently said: "My children, never do anything of which your Mother would be ashamed." Let a soul but love that Mother and he will love her Divine Son Jesus, Who, in order to make satisfaction for the unlawful pleasure of the flesh, surrendered to us His last and lawful attachment—His Mother.

The psychology of this enthusiasm for a higher love of Jesus and Mary as an escape from the unlawful attachments of the flesh is this: By it we avoid undue concentration on lower loves and their explosions. Think about your mouth for five minutes and you will have an undue concentration of saliva. Think about your heart for five minutes and you will believe you have heart trouble, though the chances are nine out of ten that you have not. Stand on a stage and think about your hands and they will begin to feel as big as hams. The balance and equilibrium of the whole system is disturbed when an organ is isolated from its function in the whole organism, or divorced from its higher purpose.

These people who are always talking, reading, and thinking about sex are like singers who think more about their larynx than about singing. They make that which is subordinate to a higher purpose so all important that the harmony of life is upset.

But suppose that instead of concentrating on an organ, one fitted that organ into a pattern of living—then all the uneasiness would end. The skilled orator never feels his hands are awkward because, being enthused about his speech, he makes the hands subordinate to their higher purpose. Our Lord practically said the same thing: "Don't worry about what you shall eat." So it is with the flesh. Cultivate a higher love, a purpose of living, a goal of existence, a desire to correspond to all that God wants us to be, and the lower passion will be absorbed by it. The Church applies this psychology to the vow of chastity. The Church asks her priests and nuns to surrender even the lawful pleasures of the flesh, not because she does not want them to love, but because she wants them to love better. She knows that their love for souls will be greater as their love for the flesh is less, just as Our Lord died on the Cross for men because He loved His Own life less.

Nor must it be thought that the vow of chastity is a burden. Thompson has called it a "passionless passion, a wild tranquility." And so it is. A new passion is born with the vow of chastity, the passion for the love of God. It is the consolation of that higher love which makes the surrender of the lower love so easy. And only when that higher love is lost does the vow begin to be a burden, just as honesty becomes a burden only to those who have lost the sense of others' rights.

The reason why there is a degeneration in the moral order and a decay of decency is because men and women have lost the higher love. Ignoring Christ their Savior, Who loved them unto His death on Calvary, and Mary who loved them unto becoming Queen of Martyrs beneath that Cross, they have nothing for which to make the sacrifice. The only way love can be shown in this world is by sacrifice, namely the surrender of one thing for another. Love is essentially bound up with choice, and choice is a negation and negation is a sacrifice. When a young man sets his heart upon a maid and asks her to marry him, he is not only saying "I choose you," he is also saying "I do not choose, I reject all others. I give them all up for you." Apply this to the problem of lust. Take away all love above flesh, take away God, the Crucifix, the Sorrowful Mother, salvation, eternal happiness—and what possibility is there for choice, what is to be gained by denying the imperious and revolutionary demands of the flesh? But grant the Divine, and the flesh's greatest joy is to throw itself on the altar of the one loved where it counts its sorrow a cheap price for the blissful joy of giving. Then its greatest despair is not to be needed; it could almost find it in its heart to inflict a wound that it might bind and heal. Such is the attitude of the pure: They have integrated their flesh with the Divine, they have sublimated its cravings with the Cross; having a higher love, they now make the surrender of the lower, that their Mother may never be put to shame.

Mary is the refuge of sinners. She who is Virgin Most Pure is also the Refuge of Sinners. She knows what sin is, not by the experience of its falls, not by tasting its bitter regrets, but by seeing what it did to her Divine Son. She looked upon His torn and bleeding flesh hanging from Him like rays of a purple sunset—and she came to know how much flesh sinned by seeing what His flesh suffered. What better way in all the world was there to measure the heinousness of sin than by seeing when left alone with Him for three hours what it could do to Innocence and Purity.

She is the Refuge of Sinners not only because she knows sin through Calvary, but also because she chose, during the most terrifying hours of her life, a converted sinner as her companion. The measure of our appreciation of friends is our desire to have them about us in the moment of greatest need. Mary heard Jesus say: "Tax collectors and prostitutes are entering the Kingdom of God ahead of you." So she chose the absolved harlot, Magdalen, as her companion at the Cross. What the scandal-mongers of that day must have said when they saw Our Blessed Mother in the company of a woman who everyone knew was the kind who sold her body without giving away her soul. Magdalen knew that day why Mary is the Refuge of Sinners, and certainly our day too can learn that if she had Magdalen as a companion then, she is willing to have us as companions now.

Mary's purity is not a "holier than thou" purity, a standoffish holiness which gathers up its robes lest they be stained by the sinful; nor is it a despising purity which looks down upon the impure. Rather it is a radiating purity which is no more spoiled by solicitude for the fallen than a ray of sunshine is sullied by a dirty window pane through which it pours.

There is no reason for the fallen being discouraged. Hope is the message of Golgotha. Find a higher love than the flesh, a love pure, understanding, redeeming, and the struggle will be easy. That higher love is on the Cross and beneath it. We almost seem to forget that there is a Cross at all. He begins to look more like a red rose and she begins to look like the stem. That stem reaches down from Calvary into all our wounded hearts of earth, sucking up our prayers and petitions and conveying them to Him. That is why roses have thorns in this life—to keep away every disturbing influence that might destroy our union with Jesus and Mary.

If Christ should come on earth some summer
    day
And walk unknown upon our busy streets,
I wonder how 'twould be if we should meet,
And being God—if He would act that way.

Perhaps the kind of thing that He would do
Would be just to forget I failed to pray
And clasp my hand forgivingly, and say,
"My child, I've heard My mother speak of
    you."

(Mrs. Frederick V. Murphy)

IV

THE FOURTH WORD: PRIDE

"My God, my God, why have You forsaken me?"

The Fourth Word from the Cross was in reparation for the sin of Pride. Pride is an inordinate love of one's own excellence, either of body or mind or the unlawful pleasure we derive from thinking we have no superiors. Pride being swollen egoism, it erects the human evil into a separate center of originativeness apart from God; exaggerates its own importance, and becomes a world in and for itself. All other sins are evil deeds, but pride insinuates itself even into good works to destroy and slay them. For that reason Sacred Scripture says: "Pride goes before the fall."

Pride manifests itself in many forms: *atheism,* which is a denial of our dependence on God, our Creator and our final end; *intellectual vanity,* which makes minds unteachable because they think they know all there is to know; *superficiality,* which judges others by their clothes, their accent, and their bank account; *snobbery,* which sneers at inferiors as the earmark of its own superiority, "they are not of our social status"; *vain-glory,* which prompts some Catholic parents to refuse to send their boys and girls to Catholic colleges, because they would there associate only with the children of carpenters; *presumptuousness,* which inclines a man to seek honors and positions quite beyond his capacity; and *exaggerated sensitiveness* which makes one incapable of moral improvement because so unwilling to hear one's own faults.

Pride it was that made Satan fall from heaven and man fall from grace. By its very nature such undue self-exaltation could be cured only by self-humiliation. That is why He who might have been born in a palace by the Tiber as befitting His Majesty as the Son of God, chose to appear before men in a stable as a child wrapped in swaddling bands. Added to this humility of His birth was the humility of His profession—a carpenter in an obscure village of Nazareth whose name was a reproach among the great. Just as today there are those who sneer at the humble walks of life, so too there were then those who jibed: "Is this not the carpenter's son?" There was also the humility of His actions, for never once did He work a miracle in His own behalf, not even to supply Himself with a place to lay His head.

Humility of example there was too, when on Holy Thursday night He who is the Lord of heaven and earth girds Himself with a towel, gets down on His knees, and with basin and water washes the twenty-four calloused feet of His Apostles saying: "The servant is not greater than his lord.... If I, *your* Lord and Teacher, have washed your feet, you too should wash each other's feet." Finally, there was humility of precept: "Unless you be converted, and become as little children, you shall not enter into the Kingdom of Heaven."

But the supreme humiliation of all was the manner of death He chose, for "He humbled Himself... even to death, death on a cross." To atone for false pride of ancestry: He thrusts aside the consolation of Divinity; for pride of popularity: He is laughed to scorn as He hangs cursed upon a tree; for pride of snobbery: He is put in the company of thieves; for pride of wealth: He is denied even the ownership of His own deathbed; for pride of flesh: "there was no beauty in him"; for pride in influential friends: He is forgotten even by those whom He cured; for pride of power: He is weak and abandoned; for pride of those who surrender God and their faith: He wills to feel without God. For all the egotism, false independence, and atheism: He now offers satisfaction by surrendering the joys and consolations of His Divine Nature. Because proud men forgot God, He permits Himself to feel Godlessness and it broke His heart in the saddest of all cries: "My God, my God, why have You forsaken me?" There was union even in the separation; but they were words of desolation uttered that we might never be without consolation.

Two lessons emerge from this Word: (1) Glory not in ourselves for God resists the proud; and (2) Glory in humility for humility is truth and the path to true greatness.

Why should we be proud? As St. Paul reminds us "What do you have that you didn't receive? And if you received it, why do you boast, as if it were your own?" Is it our voice, our wealth, our beauty, our talents of which we are proud? But what are these but gifts of God, anyone of which He might revoke this second? From a material point of view, we are worth so little. The content of a human body is equivalent to as much iron as there is in a nail, as much sugar as there is in two lumps, as much oil as there is in seven bars of soap, as much phosphorus as there is in 2200 matches, and as much magnesium as it takes to develop one photograph. In all, the human body, chemically, is worth a little less than two dollars—"O why should any mortal spirit be proud?" But *spiritually* we are worth more than the universe: "For what profit is there if one gains the whole world and loses himself in the process? What could one give in exchange for his soul?"

God resists the proud. The Pharisee who praised

his own good deeds in the forefront of the temple is condemned; the poor publican in the rear of the temple, who calls himself a sinner and strikes his breast in a plea for pardon, goes to his house justified. The harlots and the publicans who are conscious of their sin enter the Kingdom of Heaven before the Scribes and the Pharisees, who are conscious of their righteousness. The Heavenly Father is thanked for concealing His Wisdom from the self-wise and the conscious intellectuals and for revealing it to the simple: "I praise You, Father, Lord of heaven and earth, because You hid these things from the wise and the learned and revealed them to these little ones." I am sure that anyone who has had experience with the proud will bear witness to the truth of this statement: If my own eternal salvation were conditioned upon saving the soul of one self-wise man who prided himself on his learning, or one hundred of the most morally corrupt men and women of the streets, I should choose the easier task of converting the hundred. Nothing is more difficult to conquer in all the world than intellectual pride. If battleships could be lined with it instead of with armor, no shell could ever pierce them.

This is easy to understand, for if a man thinks he knows it all, then—he thinks—there is nothing left for him to know, not even what God might tell him. If the soul is filled to the brim with the ego, there is no place left for God. If a vessel is filled with water it cannot also be filled with oil. So it is with the soul. God can give His Truth and Life only to those who have emptied themselves. We must create a vacuum in our own souls in order to make room for grace. We live under the impression that we do more than we actually do. Take, for example, the simple fact of drinking liquid through a straw. We erroneously believe that we draw up the liquid through the straw. We do not, for strictly speaking there is no such thing as suction. All that we do is create a vacuum; the atmosphere presses down on the liquid with a weight equal to that of an ocean covering the earth to a depth of thirty-four feet. It is this pressure that pushes the liquid up through the straw when we create the vacuum. So too in our spiritual lives. The good we accomplish is not through the action of ourselves, as much as it is through the spiritual pressure of God's grace. All that we have to do is create a vacuum, to count ourselves as nothing— and immediately God fills the soul with His Power and Truth. The paradox of the apostolate is, then: the less we think we are, the more good we do. It was only when Peter had labored all night long and taken nothing, that Our Lord filled his boat with the miraculous draught of fishes. The higher the building the deeper the foundation; the greater the virtue the more the humility. God's instruments for good in the world are for that reason only the humble; reducing themselves to zero they leave room for infinity, whereas those who think themselves infinite, God leaves with their little zero.

Even in the world we find a natural basis for humility. As long as we are small, everything else seems big. A boy mounts a broomstick which is no more than four feet long and yet to him it is a Pegasus traveling through space; he can hear the hoofs beating the clouds as he clings to the "whistling mane of every wind." His world is peopled with giants because he is so little; tin soldiers to him are real soldiers fighting real battles and the red of the carpet is the blood of the battle field. When he grows to be a big man, the giants shrink in size; the horses become broomsticks and the soldiers are painted tin no more than three inches high. In the spiritual order, it is the same; as long as there is a God who is wiser than we, greater than we, more powerful than we, then the world is a house of wonders. Truth is then something so vast that not even an eternity can sound its depths. Love then is so abiding that not even heaven can dull its ecstasies. Goodness becomes so profound that thanks must ever be on one's lips. But just forget God, make yourself a god, and then your little learning is your title to omniscience. Then the saints become for you "stupid fools"; the martyrs, "fanatics"; the religious, "dumb"; confession, a "priestly invention"; the Eucharist, a "vestige of paganism"; heaven, a "childish fancy"; and truth, a "delusion." It must be wonderful to know so much, but it must be terrible to find out in the end that one really knows so little.

The second lesson to be derived from this Fourth Word from the Cross is that humility is truth. Humility is not an underestimation of our talents or gifts or powers, nor is it their exaggeration. A man who is six feet tall is not humble if he says he is only five feet four inches tall, just as he is not humble if he says he is seven feet tall. Humility is truth or the recognition of gifts as gifts, faults as faults. Humility is dependence on God as pride is independence of Him. It was that sense of independence or being without God which wrung out of the heart of Our Lord on the Cross this pitiable cry of abandonment: "My God, my God, why have You forsaken me?" The humble soul, conscious of his dependence on God, is always the thankful soul. How many singers, orators, musicians, actors, doctors, professors ever think of thanking God for the special talents which made them outstanding in their profession? Out of the ten lepers who were made clean only one returned to give thanks. "Were not ten made clean? Where are the other nine?", probably represents the proportion of the ungrateful who thank not because they are not humble. The humble soul will always avoid praising his own good works and thus making void the virtues of his deeds. Self-praise devours merit; and those who have done good things to be seen by men, and who trumpet their philanthropies in the market places, will one day hear the saddest words of tongue or pen: "You have already had your reward." The humble man, even though he be great in the eyes of the world, will esteem himself less than others, for he will always suspect that their internal greatness may far overreach his insignificant external greatness. He will therefore not flaunt his accidental superiority before his fellowman, for to do so is to prove one is not truly great. The really big men are the humble men; they are always approachable, kind, and understanding. It is the little men who must put on airs. The really rich boy need not wear good clothes to impress his friends with his wealth, but the poor boy must do so to create the false impression of wealth. So it is with those who have nothing in their heads; they must be eternally creating the impression of how much they know, the books they have read, and the university from which they were graduated. The learned man never has to "seem" learned, as the saint never has to appear pious—but the hypocrite does. The fact that so many men take honors seriously, change their voices, and cultivate poses, proves they never should have had the honors—the honors were too big for them. They could not assimilate the honors; rather the honors assimilated them. Instead of wearing purple, the purple wears them. A sponge can absorb so much water and no more; a character can absorb so much praise and no more; the point of saturation is reached when the honor ceases to be a part of him and begins to stick out like a sore thumb. The truly great are like St. Philip Neri who one day, seeing a criminal being led off to prison, said: "There, except for the grace of God, goes Philip Neri."

Suppose we began to be humble and esteemed others at least no less than ourselves. Suppose to those who wounded us with their slanderous darts, we answered: "Father, forgive!" Suppose to those who classified us with thieves, we made the best of it and converted them saying: "This day, Paradise." Suppose out of those who shamed us before relatives, as Jesus was shamed before His Mother, we made a new friend for our heavenly Mother: "Behold your son!" Suppose to those beneath us in worldly dignity we humbled ourselves and asked them for a drink: "I thirst!" Suppose we began to be truthful, and estimated ourselves at our real worth. If we did these things for but one hour, we would completely revolutionize the world. We are not wanting an example for we have before our eyes Him Who humbled Himself to death on the Cross, Who surrendered Divine consolation as Power put on the rags of weakness and Strength girded itself in abandonment, and, being God, appeared to be without God. And why did He do this? Because you and I have been trying to lead our lives without God—to be independent. By choosing the humiliation of the

Cross in reparation for pride He takes us back again to the story of David and Goliath.

Goliath was a great giant clothed in an armor of steel and carrying in his hand a mighty sword. David was the shepherd boy without defensive steel and carrying no other weapon than a staff, and five little stones from a nearby brook. Goliath scorned him, saying: "Am I a dog, that you have come out to me with a staff?" David answered humbly, not trusting in his own power: "I come to you in the name of the Lord…." The outcome we know. The boy with a stone killed the giant with the armor and sword.

The victory of David symbolized the reality of Good Friday. Pride is Goliath. Our Lord is the humble David who comes to slay pride with the staff of His Cross and five little stones—five wounds, in hands, feet, and side. With no other weapon than these five wounds and the staff of the Cross do we gain victories over the Goliath of pride on the battlefield of our soul. To the worldly they seem ill-fitted for battle, and impotent to conquer, but not if we understand God's plan from the beginning that: "…the foolish things of the world God has chosen, that He may confound the wise; and the weak things of the world God has chosen that He may confound the strong." It was with a cross and a crowned brow that God won the day.

O smitten mouth! O forehead crowned with
       thorn!
    O chalice of all common miseries!
Thou for our sakes that loved thee not has
       borne
    An agony of endless centuries,
And we were vain and ignorant nor knew
That when we stabbed thy heart it was our
       own real hearts we slew.

Being ourselves the sowers and the seeds,
    The night that covers and the lights that
       fade,
The spear that pierces and the side that bleeds,
    The lips betraying and the life betrayed;
The deep hath calm: the moon hath rest: but
       we
Lords of the natural world are yet our own
       dread enemy.

Nay, nay, we are but crucified, and though
    The bloody sweat falls from our brows like
       rain,
Loosen the nails—we shall come down I
       know,
    Stanch the red wounds—we shall be whole
       again,
No need have we of hyssop-laden rod,
That which is purely human, that is Godlike,
       that is God.

(Oscar Wilde)

V

THE FIFTH WORD: GLUTTONY

"I thirst."

The Fifth Word from the Cross was in reparation for the sin of Gluttony. Gluttony is an inordinate indulgence in food or drink, and may manifest itself either in taking more than is necessary, or in taking it at the wrong time, or in taking it too luxuriously. It is sinful because reason demands that food and drink be taken for the necessities and conveniences of nature but not for pleasure alone. The Gospel describes Dives as being guilty of this sin. There is no mention in the story given to us by Our Blessed Lord that Dives was a wicked man. We have no record of him ever underpaying his servants or of being guilty of any moral turpitude. Our Lord tells us only that he was "clothed in purple and fine linen, and feasted sumptuously every day." Then Our Lord continues: "A certain poor man named Lazarus used to lay at his gate, covered with sores, and he longed to fill himself with what fell from the rich man's table; why, even the dogs used to come and lick his sores. Now it happened that the poor man died and was carried away by the angels to the bosom of Abraham. The rich man also died and was buried, and in Hades when he lifted his eyes—he was in torments—he saw Abraham afar off, and Lazarus in his bosom. And he called out and said: 'Father Abraham, have mercy on me and send Lazarus to dip the tip of his finger in water to cool my tongue; for I am in great pain in these flames!' But Abraham said to him, 'My child, remember that you received good things during your lifetime, and Lazarus bad things, but now he is being comforted here while you are in pain. Besides, a yawning chasm has been placed between you and us, so that those who wish to cross over from here to you are unable to, nor can anyone cross over from there to us.' Then the rich man said: 'Then, father, I beg you to send him to my father's house, for I have five brothers, to solemnly warn them so that they won't come to this place of torment, too.' But Abraham said to him, 'They have Moses and the prophets; let them listen to *them*.' 'Oh, no, father Abraham!' he said. 'but if someone came to them from the dead, they'd repent.' But Abraham said to him: 'If they won't listen to Moses and the prophets, they won't be convinced even if someone rises from the dead.'"

If there is any indication of the present degeneration of society better than another it is the excess of luxury in the modern world. When men begin to forget their souls, they begin to take great care of their bodies. There are more athletic clubs in the modern world than there are spiritual retreat houses; and who shall count the millions spent in beauty shops to glorify faces that will one day be the prey of worms. It is not particularly difficult to find thousands who will spend two or three hours a day in exercising, but if you ask them to bend their knees to God in five minutes of prayer they protest that it is too long. Added to this is the shocking amount that is yearly spent, not in the normal pleasure of drinking, but in its excess. The scandal increases when one considers the necessary wants of the poor which could have been supplied by the amount spent for such dehumanization. The Divine judgment upon Dives is bound to be repeated upon many of our generation, who will find that the beggars for whose service they refused to interrupt their luxuries, will be seated at the Banquet of the King of Kings, while they, like Dives, will be the beggars for but a drop of water.

Some reparation had to be made for gluttony, drunkenness, and excessive luxury. That reparation began at the birth of Our Lord when He Who might have pulled down the heavens for His housetop and the stars for His chandeliers, chose to be rejected by men and driven as an outcast to a cave in the hillsides of the least of the cities of Israel. The very first sermon He preached was a plea for detachment: "Blessed are the poor in spirit, for theirs is the kingdom of heaven." He began His public life by fasting forty days and bade men, "Do not worry about your life, what you'll eat, or about your body, what you'll wear; Is not life more than food and the body more than clothing?" Traveling about as an itinerant prophet, He admitted He was as homeless as at His birth and that the beasts and the birds had a better habitation than He: "The foxes have lairs, and the birds of the air have nests; but the Son of Man has nowhere to lay His head." There was no luxury in the way He dined, for we know of one meal which He Himself prepared and it consisted only of bread and fish.

Finally, at the Cross He is stripped of His garments and denied a deathbed, in order to go out of His own world as He came into it—Lord of it and yet possessing nothing. The waters of the sea were His and all the fountains of the earth had sprung up at His word; He it was who drew the bolt of Nature's waterfalls and shut up the seas with doors; He it was who said: "Everyone who drinks this water will thirst again. But whoever drinks the water I will give him will never thirst; instead, the water I will give him will become a spring of water welling up in him to eternal life." "If anyone thirst, let him come to Me and drink." But now He lets fall from His lips the shortest of the seven cries from the Cross and the one which expresses the keenest of all human sufferings in reparation for those who have had their fill: "I thirst."

A soldier immediately put a sponge full of vinegar on a stick and pressed it to His lips. Thus was fulfilled the prophecy uttered by the Psalmist a thousand years before: "In my thirst they gave me vinegar to drink." He Who fed the birds of the air is left unfed; He Who changed water into wine, now thirsts; the everlasting fountains are dry; the God-man is poverty stricken. The Divine Lazarus stands at the door of the world and begs for a crumb and a drop, but the door of generosity is closed in His face.

Thus was reparation made for the luxury of eating and drinking. When Mirabeau was dying he called for opium, saying, "You promised to spare me needless suffering.... Support this head, the greatest head in France." When Christ is dying, He refuses the drug to alleviate His suffering. He deliberately wills to feel the most poignant of human wants, that He might balance in the scales of justice those who had more than they needed. He even made Himself the least of all men by asking them for a drink—not a drink of earthly water. That is not what He wanted; but a drink for His thirsty heart—a drink of love: *I thirst for love!*

This word from the Cross reveals that there is

a double hunger and a double thirst: one of the body, the other of the soul. On many previous occasions Our Lord had distinguished between them: "Woe to you who are filled, for you shall hunger. Woe to you who laugh now, for you shall mourn and weep." "Blessed are you who hunger now, for you shall have your fill. Blessed are you who weep now, for you shall be consoled." Then to the multitude who followed Him across the sea in search of bread, He said: "Labor not for food that perishes but for food that remains for life eternal, which the Son of Man will give you." To the Samaritan woman who came to draw water at Jacob's well, He foretold: "Everyone who drinks this water will thirst again; but whoever drinks the water I shall give him will never thirst forever. Instead the water I will give him will become a spring of water welling up in him to eternal life." But above all other references to the food and drink of the inner man as contrasted with that of the outer man, He promised the supreme nourishment of Himself: "For My flesh is food indeed, and My blood is drink."

It is in the light of this double hunger and thirst of body and soul that the distinction between dieting and fasting becomes clear. The Church fasts; the world diets. Materially there is no difference, for a person can lose twenty pounds one way as well as the other. But the difference is in the intention. The Christian fasts not for the sake of the body, but for the sake of the soul; the pagan fasts not for the sake of the soul, but for the sake of the body. The Christian does not fast because he believes the body is wicked, but in order to make it pliable in the hands of the soul, like a tool in the hands of a skilled workman. That brings us down to the basic problem of life. Is the soul the tool of the body, or the body the tool of the soul? Should the soul do what the body wants, or should the body do what the soul wants? Each has its appetites and each is imperious in the satisfaction of its wants. If we please one, we displease the other, and vice versa. Both of them cannot sit down together at the banquet of life.

The development of character depends upon which hunger and thirst we cultivate. To diet or to fast—that is the problem. To lose a double chin in order to be more beautiful in the eyes of creatures or to lose it in order to keep the body tamed and ever obedient to the spiritual demands of the soul—that is the question. Human worth can be judged by human desires. Tell me your hungers and your thirsts and I will tell you what you are. Do you hunger for money more than mercy, for riches more than virtue, and for power more than service? Then you are selfish, pampered, and proud. Do you thirst for the Wine of Everlasting Life more than for pleasure, and for the poor more than the favor of the rich, and for souls more than for the first places at table? Then you are a humble Christian.

The great pity is that so many have been so concerned with the body that they neglect the soul, and in neglecting the soul they lose the appetite for the spiritual. Just as it is possible in the physiological order for a man to lose all appetite for food, so it is possible in the spiritual order to lose all desire for the supernatural. Gluttonous about the perishable, they become indifferent to the everlasting. Like deaf ears which are dead to the environment of harmony and blind eyes which are dead to the environment of beauty, so warped souls become dead to the environment of the Divine. Darwin tells us in his autobiography that in his love for the biological he lost all the taste which he once had for poetry and music, and he regretted the loss all the days of his life. Nothing so much dulls the capacity for the spiritual as excessive dedication to the material. Excessive love of money destroys a sense of value; excessive love of the flesh kills the values of the spirit. Then comes a moment when everything seems to rebel against the higher law of our being. As the poet has put it: "All things betrayest thee, who betrayest Me." Nature is so loyal to its Maker that it is always in the end disloyal to those who abuse it. "Traitorous trueness and loyal deceit" is its best poetic description, for in faithfulness to Him it will always be fickle with us.

The Fifth Word from the Cross is God's plea to the human heart to satisfy itself at the only satisfying fountain. God cannot compel men to thirst for the holy in place of the base, or for the divine rather than the secular; that is why His plea is merely an affirmation. "I thirst," meaning I thirst to be thirsted for. And His thirst is our salvation.

A twofold recommendation is hidden in this short sermon from the Cross: first, to mortify bodily hunger and thirst; and second, to cultivate a spiritual hunger and thirst.

We are to *mortify bodily hunger and thirst* not because the flesh is wicked, but because the soul must ever exercise mastery over it, lest it become a tyrant. Quite apart from avoiding all excesses, the Cross commits us even to the minimizing of expenditures for luxuries, for the sake of the poor. How many ever think of foregoing an elaborate dinner and theater party, or a debut, out of genuine sympathy and affection for Christ's poor? Dives did not, and he lost his soul because of that forgetfulness. How many in less ample circumstances even mortify themselves one movie a month in order to drop its equivalent in the poor box, that He who sees in secret may reward in secret? The Divine counsel concerning such restraint of bodily appetites is unmistakable. On one occasion when Our Lord was invited to the home of the Prince of the Pharisees, He addressed the host himself saying: "When you give a meal or feast, call neither your friends, nor your brothers, nor your kinsmen, no rich neighbors, lest they also invite you in turn and repay you. Instead, when you throw a banquet, invite the poor, the crippled, the lame and the blind, and you will be blessed because they won't have anything to repay you with—you'll be repaid at the resurrection of the just!"

The money we spend in the excesses of bodily hunger and thirst will do us no good on the last day; but the poor whom we have assisted by our restraint and mortification will stand up as so many advocates before the bar of Divine Justice, and will plead for mercy on our souls, even though they once were heavily laden with sin. The Heavenly Judge cannot be bought with money, but He can be swayed by the poor. On that last day, the only one which really counts, will be fulfilled the beautifully prophetic words of the Mother of Our Lord: "He has filled the hungry with good things; and the rich he has sent empty away." When such surrenders of the superfluous food and drink are made for the soul's sake, let it all be done in a spirit of joy. "When you fast, don't be gloomy like the hypocrites. They make their faces unsightly to let others see that they are fasting. Amen I say to you, they have received their full reward. But when you fast anoint your head and wash your face, so others won't see that you are fasting, but only your Father Who is hidden will see; and your Father Who sees what is hidden will reward you."

We are, in addition, to *cultivate a spiritual hunger and thirst.* Mortification of the bodily appetites is only a means, not an end. The end is union with God, the soul's desire. "Taste and see that the Lord is sweet." The great tragedy of life is not so much what people have suffered, but what they have missed. It comes but within the compass of a pen to satisfy their earthly desires with wealth, but there is no one living, who, if he or she willed it, could not enjoy the spiritual food and drink which God serves to all who ask. And yet how few there are who ever think of nourishing their souls. How few there must have been in Jerusalem to have drawn from Our Lord the sweet complaint: "How often I wanted to gather together your children, like a hen gathers her brood under her wings, but you would not!" Well indeed might the Savior say to us as we listen to the cry: "I thirst" the words He addressed to the woman at the well, "If you but knew the gift of God, and Who it is Who is saying to you, 'Give Me a drink,' you would have asked Him and He would have given you living water."

But how many ask? Consider the greatest gift of God to men: the Bread of Life and the Wine that germinates virgins. How few avail themselves of the Divine Presence to break their fast each morning on the Heavenly food of the soul! How many are sufficiently conscious that Our Lord is present in the tabernacle to pay a daily visit to Him in His Prison of

Love? And if we do not, what does it witness to but the deadening of our spiritual sense? Our body would miss a dessert more than our soul would miss a Communion.

No wonder Our Crucified Redeemer thirsted for us on the Cross—thirsted for our unresponsive hearts and dulled souls. Nor let us think that His thirst is a proof of His need, but of our own. He does not need us for His perfection any more than we need the flower that blooms outside our window for our perfection. In dry seasons we desire rain for the flower, not because we need the rain, but because the flower needs it. In like manner, God thirsts for us not because He needs us for His happiness, but because we need Him for our happiness.

Without Him it is impossible for us to develop. Just as certain diseases, such as rickets and anemia, arise in the body from a deficiency of necessary vitamins, so too our characters fail because of a deficiency of the Spirit. The vast majority of men and women in the world today are so underdeveloped spiritually that if a like deficiency showed in their bodies they would be physical monstrosities. How many millions of minds there are today that are devoid of one single satisfying truth which they can carry through life to sustain them in their sorrows and console their death? How many millions of wills there are that have not yet found the goal of life and which, because they are presently without it, flit like butterflies from one colored emotion to another, unable to find repose?

Let them cultivate a taste for something more than bread and circuses; let them sound the depths of their beings to discover there the arid wastes crying for the refreshment of everlasting fountains. Of course these emaciated hungry souls are not altogether to blame. They have heard preachers without end preaching *Go to Christ!* But what does that mean? Go back some 2000 years? If so, then have they not a right to doubt the Divinity of Him who could not project Himself through time? Look up to heaven? If so, then what has become of His blessing, His forgiveness of sinners, His Truth that He said would endure unto the end of time? Where is His authority? His power? His Life now? If it is not some place on earth, then why did He come to earth? To leave only the echo of His words, the record of His deeds, and then to slip away leaving us only a history and its teachers?

Somewhere on earth today is His Truth: "He who hears you, hears Me." Somewhere on earth is His Power: "Behold, I have given you power...." Somewhere on earth is His Life: "The bread that I will give is My flesh for the life of the world." Where find it? There is an institution on the face of the earth which claims to be that, and to those who have knocked at its portals and have asked for a drink has come the elixir of Divine Life and with it the peace which comes to those who drink and never thirst again, and eat and never hunger again.

To each and everyone of us, inside and outside the Church, Our Lord asks: "Will you accept the cup of My Love?" He took our cup of hate and bitterness in Gethsemane and its dregs were so bitter they made Him cry out: "My Father, if it be possible, let this chalice pass from Me." But He drank every drop of it. If He drank our cup of hates why do we not drink His chalice of pardon? Why then, when He cries, "I thirst," do we hand Him vinegar and gall?

> I cannot tell the half of it, yet hear
> What rush of feeling still comes back to me,
> From that proud torture hanging on His
>   Cross,
> From that gold rapture of His Heart in mine.
>
> I knew in blissful anguish what it means
> To be a part of Christ, and feel as mine
> The dark distresses of my brother limbs,
> To feel it bodily and simply true,
> To feel as mine the starving of His poor,
> To feel as mine the shadow of curse on all,
> Hard words, hard looks, and savage misery,
> And struggling deaths, unpitied and unwept.
> To feel rich brothers' sad satieties
> The weary manner of their lives and deaths,
> That want in love, and lacking love lack all.
> To feel the heavy sorrow of the world
> Thicken and thicken on to future hell,

To mighty cities with their miles of streets,
Where men seek work for days, and walk and
    starve,
Freezing on river-banks on winter nights,
And come at last to cord or stream or steel.

The horror of the things our brothers bear!
It was but naught to that which after came,
The woe of things we make our brothers bear,
Our brothers and our sisters! In my heart
Christ's Heart seemed beating, and the world's
    whole sin,—
Its crimson malice and grey negligence,—
Rose up and blackening hid the Face of God.

(Arthur Shearly Cripps)

VI

THE SIXTH WORD: SLOTH

"It is finished."

The Sixth Word from the Cross was in reparation for the sin of Sloth. Sloth is a malady of the will which causes us to neglect our duties. Sloth may be either physical or spiritual. It is physical when it manifests itself in laziness, procrastination, idleness, softness, indifference, and nonchalance. It is spiritual when it shows itself in an indifference to character betterment, a distaste for the spiritual, a hurried crowding of devotions, a lukewarmness and failure to cultivate new virtue. The classic description of the effects of sloth are to be found in the Book of Proverbs: "I passed by the field of the slothful man, and by the vineyard of the man without sense; And behold! it was all overgrown with thistles; its surface was covered with nettles, and its stone wall was broken down. And as I gazed at it, I reflected; I saw and learned the lesson: A little sleep, a little slumber, a little folding of the arms to rest—Then will poverty come upon you like a highwayman, and want like an armed man." Of such indifference to duty Our Lord spoke in the Book of Revelation: "But because you are lukewarm, and neither cold nor hot, I will vomit you out of My mouth."

The life and teaching of Our Lord lend no support to the slothful man. When yet only twelve years of age He speaks of being about His "Father's business" which was nothing less than redeeming the world. Then for eighteen years He worked as a manual laborer transforming dead and useless things into the child's crib, the friend's table, Nazarene roofs, and the farmer's wagons, as symbols of His later work by which He would transform hard money changers and prostitutes into useful citizens of the Kingdom of Heaven. Beginning a public life with calloused hands He preached the Gospel of work: "I must do the works of the One Who sent Me, while it is day; night is coming when no man is able to work." His whole life, in His own words, was spent not in receiving but in giving: "the Son of Man came, not come to be served, but to serve, and to give His life as a ransom for many." He earned the right to teach the necessity of work, and lest we live under any illusions that any other work is more important than the saving of souls, even the burial of our fathers, He said to the disciple who asked for such permission: "Follow Me, and let the dead bury their dead." To the young man who wished to be His disciple but first wanted to bid farewell to his friends at home, Our Lord said: "No one who puts his hand to the plough, and looks behind, is fit for the kingdom of God." Laboring for bread alone is no fulfillment of His commandment, for to those who wanted more bread He pleaded: "Labor not for food that perishes, but for food that remains for life eternal, which the Son of Man will give you."

The business of salvation is no easy task. There are two roads through this world and two gates into the future life. "Go in through the narrow gate, for wide is the gate, and broad the way leading to destruction, and many are those who enter through it. How narrow the gate and difficult the way leading to life, and few are those who find it!" Curiously enough, His invitation goes out only to those who labor for the eternal prize: "Come to Me, all you who labor and are burdened, and I will refresh you. Take My yoke upon you, and learn from Me, for I am meek and humble of heart, and you will find rest for your souls. For My yoke is easy, and My burden light."

So completely had He fulfilled the smallest detail of His Father's business that the very night of His Agony, in the Garden in the presence of His Apostles, He could raise His eyes to heaven and pray: "Father… I have glorified You on earth; I have finished the work which You gave Me to do." Then the following afternoon, as the Carpenter is put to death by His own profession, He cries out from the Cross in a loud voice the final reparation for sloth and the song of triumph: "It is finished!"

He did not say: "I die," because death did not come to take Him. He walked to it to conquer it. The last drop in the chalice of Redemption was drained; the last nail had been driven in the mansion of the Father's House; the last brush touched to the canvas of salvation! His work was done!

But ours is not. It is important to realize this for there are the slothful who justify themselves by saying they need only faith in Christ to save their souls. Surely He who worked so hard for the world's redemption came not to dispense His followers from work. The servant is not above the master. Faith in Him alone does not save, for "faith without good works is dead." It is not enough for the student to have faith in his teacher's knowledge; he must also study. It is not enough for the sick to have faith in their doctor; their organism must cooperate with him and his medicine. It is not enough to believe that Washington was the "father of our country"; we must also assume and fulfill our duties as American citizens. In like manner it is not enough to believe in Christ; we must live Christ and to some extent die Christ-like. His words permit of no equivocation: "Whoever does not take up his cross and follow Me is not worthy of Me. Whoever finds his life will lose it, and whoever loses his life for My sake will find it." St. Paul understood the labor involved in being a Christian and wrote the same message to the Romans: "For if in baptism we have become sharers in a death like His, we will also share in a resurrection like His." What He has done with His human nature, we must do with ours—plant it in the soil of the Cross and await the Resurrection of the Eternal Easter. Later on, to the Corinthians, Paul repeated it: "If you share in the suffering, so you shall also share the consolation." And St. Peter who knew so well the scandal of the Cross pleaded for joy in re-living the Cross: "Rejoice in so far as you are sharing in Christ's sufferings, so that when His glory is revealed you may rejoice and exult."

There is no hope for the spiritually slothful in these injunctions. Our Lord is the die; we must be stamped by it. He is the pattern; we must be modeled to it. The Cross is the condition; we must be nailed to it. Our Lord loved His Cross so much that He keeps its scars even in His glory. He Who had won victory over death, kept the record of its wounds. If so precious to Him, they cannot be meaningless for us. In their preservation is the reminder that we too must be signed with those signs and sealed with those seals. On Judgment Day He will say to each of us: "Show Me your hands and feet. Where are your scars of victory? Have you fought no battles for truth? Have you won no wars for goodness? Have you made no enemy of evil?" If we can prove we have been His warriors and show the scars on our apostolic hands, then we shall enjoy the peace of victory. But woe to us who come down from the Calvary of this earthly pilgrimage with hands unscarred and white!

Two lessons emerge from this Sixth Word from the Cross witnessing to His finished work and our own unfinished tasks: First, we must beware of spiritual sloth for its penalties are tremendous; and second, we must work for a complete life.

The Gospel records three instances of sloth. There were the foolish virgins, chaste but lazy. The wise virgins fill their lamps with oil and wait to hear the step of the approaching Bridegroom. The foolish virgins do not think of oil, and tired of waiting, they fall asleep. When the Bridegroom comes, the wise virgins light their lamps and welcome the Bridegroom. The foolish virgins go out to buy oil, but everybody is asleep, the shops are closed. They go back to the wedding feast, but the door is closed. They cry: "Lord, Lord open for us." But His answer is: "Amen I say to you, I do not know you!" Our Lord concludes the parable with these words: "Stay awake, therefore, because you do not know the day or the hour."

The second instance of sloth was the parable of the barren fig tree: "The next day as they were leaving Bethany, Jesus was hungry. And seeing from a distance a fig tree which had leaves on it, He went to see if He could find anything to eat. But when He came up to it, He found it had nothing but leaves because it wasn't the season for figs. And in response He said to it: 'May no one ever eat fruit from you ever again.'"

The third was the parable of the buried talent. He who received five talents earned another five; he who had received two earned another two; but he who received one hid it in the ground. Of him the lord of the servants said: "You evil and lazy servant!... Take the talent away from him and give it to the one with the ten talents. For all who have will receive, and will have more than enough; but as for the one who does not have, even what he has will be taken from him. And throw the worthless servant out into the outer darkness. There there will be weeping and gnashing of teeth."

Common to these three parables is the danger of sloth and the necessity of work. Purity without good works will not save any more than it saved the foolish virgins. Those who do nothing run the risk of losing the little that they have. In other words, it is possible to lose our souls by doing nothing. "How shall we escape if we neglect...?" We lose our souls not only by the evil we do, but also by the good we leave undone. Neglect the body and the muscles stiffen; neglect the mind and imbecility comes;

neglect the soul and ruin follows. Just as physical life is the sum of the forces which resist death, so the spiritual life is to some extent the sum of the forces which resist evil. Neglect to take an antidote for a poison in the body, and we die by our neglect. Neglect to take precaution against sin, and we die the death merely because of neglect.

Heaven is a city on a hill, hence we cannot coast into it; we have to climb. Those who are too lazy to mount can miss its capture as well as the evil who refuse to seek it. Let no one think he can be totally indifferent to God in this life and suddenly develop a capacity for Him at the moment of death. Where will the capacity for heaven come from if we have neglected it on earth? A man cannot suddenly walk into a lecture room on higher mathematics and be thrilled by its equations if all during life he neglected to develop a taste for mathematics. A heaven of poets would be a hell to those who never learned to love poetry. And a heaven of Divine Truth, Righteousness, and Justice would be a hell to those who never studiously cultivated those virtues here below. Heaven is only for those who work for heaven. If we crush every inspiration of the Divine; if we drown every Godward inspiration of the soul; if we choke every inlet to Christ—where will be our relish for God on the last day? The very things we neglected will then be the very cause of our ruin. The very things that should have ministered to our growth will then turn against us and minister to our decay.

The sun which warms the plant can under other conditions also wither it. The rain which nourishes the flower can under other conditions rot it. The same sun shines upon mud that shines upon wax. It hardens the mud but softens the wax. The difference is not in the sun, but in that upon which it shines. So it is with God. The Divine Life which shines upon a soul that loves Him, softens it into everlasting life; that same Divine Life which shines upon the slothful soul, neglectful of God, hardens it into everlasting death. Heaven and hell are in like manner both effects of Divine Goodness. Their difference comes from our reaction to that goodness, and to that extent are also our creations. Both God and man are in different senses creators of heaven and hell.

A little heed then to this word from the Cross: "It is finished." We finish our vocation as He finished His—on a cross and nowhere else. Only to the doers of the truth, and not to its preachers or its hearers, comes the reward of the crown. Doing implies the spending not of what we *have,* but of what we *are.* We need have no undue fear for our health if we work hard for the Kingdom of God; God will take care of our health if we take care of His cause. In any case, it is better to burn out than to rust out. Burning the candle at both ends for God's sake may be foolishness to the world, but it is a profitable Christian exercise—for so much better the light. Only one thing in life matters: Being found worthy of the Light of the World in the hour of His visitation. "Take heed," He said. "See that you are watchful, for you do not know when the appointed time is. It is like a man leaving on a journey. When he left his household he gave authority to his servants—each received a task—and he ordered the doorkeeper to stay awake. So stay awake, for you do not know when the lord of the household is coming, whether in the evening or in the middle of the night or at cock crow or in the morning. You do not want him to come suddenly and find you sleeping! But what I say to you I say to all—stay awake!"

Not only must we beware of spiritual sloth; we must *work* for a completed life. The important word in the struggle against sloth is "finished." The world judges us by results; Our Lord judges us by the way we fulfill and finish our appointed tasks. A good life is not necessarily a successful life. The sowers are not always the reapers. Those whom God destines only to sow receive their reward for just that, even though they never garnered a single sheaf into everlasting barns. In the parable of the talents, the reward is according to the development of potentialities and the completion of appointed duties. One day Our Lord "taking a seat opposite the offering box… watched the crowd toss money into the offering box.

Many rich people tossed in a great deal, but when one poor widow came she tossed in two small coppers, that is, about a penny. He called His disciples together and said to them, 'Amen, I say to you, this poor widow tossed in more than all the others who tossed money into the offering box—they all tossed in from their abundance, but she from her want tossed in all that she had, her whole livelihood.'" The result was trivial for the treasury, but it was infinite for her soul. She had not half done her duty, she had finished it. This is what is meant by a life completed.

In the Christian order it is not the important who are essential, nor those who do great things who are really great. A king is no nobler in the sight of God than a peasant. The head of government with millions of troops at his command is no more precious in the sight of God than a paralyzed child. The former has greater opportunities for evil, but like the widow in the Temple, if the child fulfills its task of resignation to the will of God more than the dictator fulfills his task of procuring social justice for the glory of God, then the child is greater. "God is no respecter of persons." Men and women are only actors on the stage of life. Why should he who plays the part of the rich man glory in his gold and rich table and consider himself better than him who plays the role of the beggar begging a crumb from his table? When the curtain goes down they are both men. So when God pulls down the curtain on the drama of the world's redemption, He will not ask what part we played, but only how well we played the role assigned to us. The Little Flower has said that one could save one's soul by picking up pins out of love of God. If we could create worlds and drop them into space from our finger tips, we would please God no more than by dropping a coin into a tin cup. It is not *what* is done, but *why* it is done that matters. A bootblack shining a pair of shoes inspired by a Divine motive is doing more good for this world than all the Godless conventions the world could ever convene.

It is the intention which makes the work. Duties in life are like marble, canvas, and stone. Marble becomes valuable because of the image given to it by the sculptor; canvas is ennobled by the picture of the artist; and stone is glorified by the pattern of the architect. So it is with our works. The intention gives them value as the image gives the marble value. God is not interested in what we do with our hands, or our money, or our minds, or our mouths, but with our *wills*. It is not the work but the worker that counts.

Let those who think their work has no value recognize that by fulfilling their insignificant tasks out of a love of God, those tasks assume a supernatural worth. The aged who bear the taunts of the young, the sick crucified to their beds, the ignorant immigrant in the steel mill, the street cleaner and the garbage collector, the wardrobe mistress in the theater and the chorus girl who never had a line, the unemployed carpenter and the ash collector—all these will be enthroned above dictators, presidents, kings, and cardinals if a greater love of God inspires their humbler tasks than inspires those who play nobler roles with less love.

No work is finished until we do it for the honor and glory of God. "Whether you eat or drink, or whatever else you do, do all for the glory of God." When our lease on life runs out there are two questions which will be asked. The world will ask: "How much did he leave?" The angels will ask: "How much did he bring with him?" The soul can carry much, but in its journey to the judgment seat of God it will be freighted down only with that kind of goods which a man can carry away from a ship-wreck—his good works done for the glory of God. All that we leave behind is "unfinished." All that we take with us is "finished."

May we never die too soon! This does not mean not dying young; it means not dying with our appointed tasks undone. It is indeed a curious fact that no one ever thinks of Our Lord as dying too young! That is because He finished His Father's business. But no matter how old we are when we die, we always feel there is something more to be done. Why do we feel that way, unless it is because we did not do well the tasks assigned to us? Our task may not be great; it may be only to add one stone to the Temple of God. But whatever it is, do each tiny little act in union with your Savior Who died on the Cross and you will *finish* your life. Then you will never die too young!

> But if, impatient, thou let slip thy cross,
> Thou wilt not find it in this world again,
> Nor in another; here, and here alone
> Is given thee to suffer for God's sake.
> In other words we shall more perfectly
> Serve Him and love Him, praise Him, work for
>   Him,
> Grow near and nearer Him with all delight;
> But then we shall not any more be called
> To suffer, which is our appointment here.
> Canst thou not suffer then one hour,—or two?
> If He should call thee from thy cross to-day,
> Saying, It is finished!—that hard cross of thine
> From which thou prayest for deliverance.
> Thinkest thou not some passion of regret
> Would overcome thee? Thou wouldst say, 'So
>   soon?
> Let me go back and suffer yet awhile
> More patiently;—I have not yet praised God.'
> And He might answer to thee,— 'Never more.
> All pain is done with.' Whensoe'er it comes,
> That summons that we look for, it will seem
> Soon, yea too soon. Let us take heed in time
> That God may now be glorified in us;

And while we suffer, let us set our souls
To suffer perfectly: since this alone,
The suffering, which is this world's special
    grace
May here be perfected and left behind....
Endure, Endure,—be faithful to the end!
        (Harriet Eleanor Hamilton-King)

VII

THE SEVENTH WORD: COVETOUSNESS

"Father, into Your hands I commend My spirit."

ADDRESS DELIVERED APRIL 7, 1939

Covetousness is an inordinate love of the things of this world. Such love becomes inordinate if one is not guided by a reasonable end, such as suitable provision for one's family or the future, or if one is too solicitous in amassing wealth or too parsimonious in dispensing it. The sin of covetousness includes, therefore, both the intention one has in acquiring the goods of this world and the manner of acquiring them. It is not the love of an excessive sum which is wrong, but an inordinate love of any sum. Simply because a man has a great fortune, it does not follow that he is a covetous man. A child with a few pennies might possibly be more covetous. Material things are lawful and necessary because they enable us to live according to our station in life, to mitigate suffering, to advance the Kingdom of God, and to save our souls. It is the pursuit of wealth as an end instead of as a means to the above ends, which makes a man covetous.

In this class of the covetous are to be placed the young woman who marries a divorced man for his money, the public official who accepts a bribe, the lawyer, the educator, or clergyman who sponsors radical movements for gold, the capitalist who puts profits above human rights and needs, and the labor leader who puts party power above the legitimate interests of the laborers. Covetousness is much more general in the world today than we suspect. It once was monopolized by the avaricious rich: now it is shared by the envious poor. Because a man has no money in his pockets is no proof that he is not covetous; he may be involuntarily poor with a passion for wealth far in excess of those who possess. History bears witness to the fact that every radical economic revolutionist in the history of the world has been interested in only one thing: booty. The only poor who ever attacked the rich and sought nothing for themselves were Our Lord and His followers, like St. Francis of Assisi. There are very few disinterested lovers of the poor today; most of their so-called champions do not love the poor as much as they hate the rich. They hate all the rich, but they love only those poor who will help them attain their wicked ends.

Such covetousness is ruinous for man, principally because it hardens the heart. Man becomes like that which he loves, and if he loves gold, he becomes like it—cold, hard, and yellow. The more he acquires, the more he suffers at surrendering even the least of it, just as it hurts to have a single hair pulled out even though your head is full of them. The more the sinfully rich man gets, the more he believes he is needy. He is always poor in his own eyes. The sense of the spiritual thus becomes so deadened that its most precious treasures are bartered away for the trivial increases, as Judas sold his Master for thirty pieces of silver. As St. Paul tells us: "The love of money is the root of all evil; in their desire for it some have strayed from the faith...." The Providence of God becomes less and less a reality, and if it still retains value, it is reduced to a secondary role; God is trusted as long as we have a good bank account.

When things go well we are quite willing to dispense with God, like the young man in the Gospel who came to Our Lord only because he was being deprived of some of his father's estate. "Lord, tell my brother to share the inheritance with me." It was only when economic confusion arose that the young man had recourse to the Divine. There are many in the world today who feel that the only reason for the existence of the Church is to improve the economic order and if they do not have their fill, they assail the Church for failing. Well indeed might the Church answer in the words of Our Lord: "Man, who made me judge or arbitrator over you?"

To turn man's heart away from perishable things to the eternal values of the soul, was one of the reasons for Our Lord's visit to the earth. His teaching from the beginning was not only a warning against covetousness, but a plea for a greater trust in Providence. "Don't store up treasures for yourselves on earth, where moth and rust destroy, and where thieves break in and steal. But store up treasures for yourself in heaven, where neither moth nor rust destroy, and where thieves neither break in nor steal. For where your treasure is, there will your heart be too." "Therefore, I tell you, do not worry about your life, what you shall eat, or for your body, what you shall wear. Is not life more than food, and the body more than clothing? Look at the birds of the sky—they neither sow nor reap nor gather into barns, yet your heavenly Father feeds them. Are you not worth more than they? But which of you by worrying, can add one moment to his life? And why do you worry about what you will wear? Look how the lilies of the field grow; they neither work nor spin. But I tell you, even Solomon in all his glory was not arrayed like one of these. But if God so clothes the grass of the field, which is here today and thrown into the oven tomorrow, won't He clothe you much better, O you of little faith? Do not worry, therefore, saying: 'What will we eat?' or 'What will we drink?'

or 'What will we put on?' for the Gentiles seek all those things. Your Heavenly Father knows you need all these things. Seek first the Kingdom and the will of God, and all those things will be given to you also. So don't go worrying about tomorrow—tomorrow will worry for itself. One day's evil is enough for a day."

The man who unduly loves riches is a fallen man, because of a bad exchange; he might have had heaven through his generosity, and he has only the earth. He could have kept his soul, but he sold it for material things. Camels will pass through the eyes of needles more easily than the covetous will pass through the gates of heaven. It was easy of course to condemn the rich; our world is too full of those who are doing it now. But our economic revolutionists do it because they envy wealth, not because they love poverty. It was not so with Our Divine Savior. He Who condemned Dives, and the man who ordered bigger barns the very day he died, and Who thundered that no man could serve God and Mammon, lived His Gospel. Not in a hospital, or a home, or a city, but in a stable in the fields did He bow entrance into the world He made. Not with money did He make money in the markets of exchange, but as a poor carpenter. He earned His living with the two most primitive instruments used: wood and hammer. During His three years of preaching not even a roof could He claim as His own: "The foxes have lairs, and the birds of the air have nests; but the Son of Man has nowhere to lay His head." Then at His death He had no wealth to leave; His Mother He gave to John; His body to the tomb; His blood to the earth; His garments to His executioners. Absolutely dispossessed, He is still hated, to give the lie to those who say religion is hated because of its possessions. Religion is hated because it is religion, and possessions are only the excuse and pretext for driving God from the earth. There was no quarreling about His will; there was no dispute about how His property would be divided; there was no lawsuit over the Lord of the Universe. He had given up everything in reparation for covetousness, keeping only one thing for Himself that was not a thing—His spirit. With a loud cry, so powerful that it freed His soul from His flesh and bore witness to the fact that He was giving up His life and not having it taken away, He said in farewell: "Father, into Your hands I commend My spirit." It rang out over the darkness and lost itself in the furthermost ends of the earth. The world has made all kinds of noise since to drown it out. Men have busied themselves with nothing, to shut out hearing it—but through the fog and darkness of cities, and the silence of the night, that awful cry rings within the hearing of every one who does not force himself to forget, and as we listen to it we learn two lessons:

1. The more ties we have to earth the harder will it be for us to die.

2. We were never meant to be perfectly satisfied here below.

In every friendship hearts grow and entwine themselves together, so that the two hearts seem to make only one heart with a single common thought. That is why separation is so painful: It is not so much two hearts separating, but one heart being torn asunder. When a man loves wealth inordinately, he and it grow together like a tree pushing itself in growth through the crevices of a rock. Death to such a man is a painful wrench, because of his close identification with the material. He has everything to live for, nothing to die for. As a result, he becomes at death the most destitute and despoiled beggar in the universe, for he has nothing he can take with him. He discovers too late that he did not belong to himself, but to things—for wealth is a pitiless master. It would not allow him during life to think of anything else except increasing itself. Now he discovers too late that by consecrating himself to filling his barns, he was never free to save the only thing he could carry with him to eternity: his soul. In order to acquire a part, he lost the whole; he won a fraction of the earth, now he will need only six feet of it. Like a giant tied down by ten thousand ropes to ten thousand stakes, he is no longer free to think about anything else than what he must leave. That is why death is so hard for the covetous rich.

On the contrary, as the ties to earth become lessened, the easier is the separation. Where our treasure is, there is our heart also. If we have lived for God, then death is a liberation. Earth and its possessions are the cage which confines us, and death is the opening of its door, enabling our soul to wing its way to its Beloved for which alone it had lived, and for which it only waited to die. Our powers of dispossession are greater than our powers of possession; our hands could never contain all the gold in the world, but we can wash our hands of its desire. We cannot own the world, but we can disown it. That is why the soul with the vow of poverty is more satisfied than the richest covetous man in the world, for the latter has not yet all he wants, while the religious wants nothing; in a certain sense the religious has all and is perfectly happy. It was such poverty of spirit raised to its sublimest peak which made the death of Our Lord so easy. He had no ties to earth. His treasure was with the Father and His soul followed the spiritual law of gravitation. Gold, like dirt, falls; charity, like fire, rises: "Father, into Your hands I commend My spirit."

The death of Our Lord on the Cross likewise reveals that we are meant to be perpetually dissatisfied here below. If earth were meant to be a Paradise, then He Who made it would never have taken leave of it on Good Friday. The commending of the spirit to the Father was at the same time the refusal to commend it to earth. The completion or fulfillment of life is in heaven, not on earth.

Our Lord in His last Word is saying that nowhere else can we be satisfied except in God. It is absolutely impossible for us to be perfectly happy here below. Nothing proves this more than disappointment. One might almost say the essence of life is disappointment. We look forward to a position, to marriage, to ownership, to power, to popularity, to wealth; and when we attain them we have to admit, if we are honest, that they never come up to our expectations. As children we looked forward to Christmas; when it did come and we had our fill of sweets and tested every toy or rocked every doll, and then crept into our beds, we said in our own little heart of hearts: "Somehow or other, it did not quite come up to expectations." That experience is repeated a thousand times in life.

But why is there disappointment? Because when we look forward to a future ideal, we endow it with something of the infinity of the soul. I can imagine a house with ten thousand rooms studded with diamonds and emeralds, but I shall never see one. I can imagine a mountain of gold, but I shall never see one. So with our earthly ideals. We color them with the qualities of our spiritual soul. But when they become realized, they are concrete, cabined, cribbed, confined. A tremendous dispro-portion thus arises between the ideal we conceived and the reality before us. That disproportion be-tween the infinite and the finite is the cause of disappointment. There is no escaping this fact. We have eternity in our heart, but time on our hands. The soul demands a heaven, and we get only an earth. Our eyes look up to the mountains, but they rest only on the plains. It is easier to strangle our ideals than it is to satisfy them. He who attains his earthly ideal, smashes it. To touch an ideal in this world is to destroy the ideal. "No man is a hero to his valet." We are no longer thirsty at the border of a well. The satisfaction of earthly ideals turns against us, like a cruel retort from one to whom we have paid an underhanded compliment.

But there is no reason for being pessimists or cynics. Disappointment is no proof there is no ideal, but only that it is not here. Just as we would have no eyes were there no beauties to see, and as we would have no ears were there no harmonies to hear, so we would have no appetite for the infinite were there no God to love. In Him alone is the reconciliation of the chase and the capture. Here on this earth we are buffeted between the two. The chase has its thrill for it is the pursuit of an ideal, the quest for satisfaction, and the march to victory. The capture too has its thrill for it is possession, enjoyment, and peace. But while we live in time we can never enjoy both together. The capture ends the excitement of the chase; and the chase without a capture is maddening, like having a refreshing spring withdrawn from our parched lips as we draw near to it.

How combine the chase without the ennui of capture, and the capture without losing the joy of the chase? It is impossible here below, but not in heaven, for when we attain God, we capture the Infinite, and because He is Infinite, it will take an eternity of chase to discover the undiscoverable joys of Life, Truth, Love, and Beauty.

Such is the meaning behind the last and farewell word from the Cross. Centuries ago the sun shone upon plants and trees and imprisoned within them its light and heat. Today we dig up that light and heat in coal, and as its flames mount upward we pay back our debt to the sun. So now the Divine Light, that for thirty-three years has been imprisoning itself in a human heart, goes back again to the Father, ever to remind us that only by completing a similar circuit and commending our souls to the Father, do we find the answer to the riddle of life, the end of disappointment, and the beginning of eternal peace for our eternal hearts.

Everything is disappointing except the Redemptive Love of Our Lord. You can go on acquiring things but you will be poor until your soul is filled with the love of Him Who died on the Cross for you. As the eye was made for seeing and the ear for hearing, so your spirit was made to be re-commended back again to God. If it had any other destiny the dying words of the Savior would have betrayed that destiny. The spirit has a capacity for the infinite; the knowledge of one flower, the life of a single hour, the love of a minute, do not exhaust its potencies; it wants the fullness of these things—in a word, it wants God.

The tragedy of our modern life is that so many put their pleasures in *desires* rather than in *discovery*. Having lost the one purpose of human living, namely God, they seek substitutes in the petty things of earth. After repeated disappointments, they begin to put their happiness not in a pleasure, but in the *hunt* for it, in butterfly existences that never rest long enough at any one moment to know their inner desires; running races hoping they will never end; turning pages but never discovering the plot; knocking at doors of truth and then dashing away lest its portals be opened and they be invited in. Existence becomes a flight from peace, rather than an advance; a momentary escape from frustration instead of its sublimation in victory.

Every now and then there comes to some a light through the clouds of Calvary and the echo of the word commending a spirit to God, but instead of making a supreme effort to satisfy the goal of life, they crucify it. "But when the farmers saw the son they said to themselves, 'This is the heir; come, let us kill him and have his inheritance!' And they took hold of him, dragged him out of the vineyard and killed him." Thus do some men believe that if they could drive God from the earth the inheritance of sin would be theirs without remorse; and if they could but silence conscience, they could inherit peace without justice. It was just this other mentality which sent Our Lord to the Cross. If the voice of God could be stifled, they believed they could enjoy the voice of Satan in peace.

Now, take a different outlook on the world. How many, even of those who have killed conscience, can say: "I am happy; there is nothing more I want"? But if you are not brave enough to say that, then why not seek? And why not seek in the one direction in which you know happiness lies? At death you will leave *everything;* but there is one thing you will not leave—your desire for life. You want the one thing the Cross brings you: Life through death.

In its effulgence the mystery of existence becomes clear. The Cross refers to *me*, personally and individually, as if no one else in the world ever existed. On the Cross He has traced for me in sacrifice, which is the sublimest of gestures, a program of life: Submission to the Divine Will. He went down the dark road of Gethsemane to Calvary's death out of devotedness to God's glory and my salvation. For my culpable self-indulgence, He atones by surrender of Himself. "He was pierced for our offenses, crushed for our sins; upon Him was the chastisement that makes us whole...."

If this Master of the world's symphony would miss my single note of virtue in the harmony of the universe; if this Captain of wars would miss my spear in His battle for goodness; if this Artist would miss my little daub of color in the masterpiece of redemption; if this Cosmic Architect would note the absence of my little stone in the building of His temple; if this Tree of Life would feel the fall of but my little leaf to the sinfulness of earth; if this the Heavenly Father would miss me in the empty chair at the banquet spread for the millions of the children of God; if this Orator from the Pulpit of the Cross would note my inattention as I turned to glance at an executioner; if God cares that much for me, then I must be worth something since He loves me so!

> But if Himself He come to thee, and stand
> Beside thee, gazing down on thee with eyes
> That smile, and suffer; that will smite thy
>   heart,
> With their own pity, to a passionate peace;
> And reach to thee Himself and the Holy Cup
> (With all its wreathen stems of passion-flowers
> And quivering sparkles of the ruby stars),
> Pallid and royal, saying 'Drink with Me';
> Wilt thou refuse? Nay, not for Paradise!
> The pale brow will compel thee, the pure
>   hands

Will minister unto thee; thou shalt take
Of that communion through the solemn
    depths
Of the dark waters of thine agony,
With heart that praises Him, that yearns to
    Him
The closer through that hour. Hold fast His
    hand,
Though the nails pierce thine too! take only
    care
Lest one drop of the sacramental wine
Be spilled, of that which ever shall unite
Thee, soul and body to thy living Lord!

        (Harriet Eleanor Hamilton-King)

VIII

CONCLUSION: CLOSED DOORS

Only once in the history of the world was a guard ever placed before the tomb of a dead man. Only once in the scrolls of time has it ever been recorded that a stone was rolled before a sepulcher to prevent the escape of a corpse—and that was on Good Friday. If Hitler had sent his soldiers to guard the tomb of Bismarck the rest of the world would have taken it as the maddest of all mad acts. If the French Republic had thrown a circle of armored cars about the tomb of Napoleon and sealed its entrance with a mammoth stone, the world would have laughed France to scorn.

And yet here, in all seriousness, after a Man had been buffeted, crowned with thorns, scourged until His flesh hung from Him like crimsoned ribbons, loaded down with a heavy tree which He was forced to drag through city streets and up a hill, carpentered to it by members of His own profession, then hung from steel pegs for three hours, pierced with a lance until blood and water poured forth, found dead and then buried in a suffocating hundred weight of spices—after all this, the chief priests and Pharisees go to the Roman Governor and ask authorization to "seal the stone and station a guard."

These precautions have never struck the world as humorous, though under all other circumstances it would be the height of ridiculousness to see swords drawn and soldiers at attention before a sealed tomb of a dead man. The spectacle of hunters shrinking in terror from a dead lion or of zoologists vaccinating themselves in the presence of a dead serpent, would not be such folly as the spectacle of men standing poised to resist the onslaught of the dead.

What deprives this scene of the note of stupidity is that His enemies were really fearful that He would rise again. They called Him an "impostor" and yet they feared He was not; they asked Him to "come down" from the Cross and they were half afraid He actually would; they ridiculed His Prophecy that He would rise again on the third day, but they sealed the door of the sepulcher because they feared He might rise; they laughed Him to scorn when He said no other sign would be given an incredulous generation than the sign of Jonah, and yet they asked for Roman soldiers to stand guard over the whale of the earth lest it deliver itself of its burden upon the shores of eternity. They were sure

He was buried and yet they were not sure His life would be taken away; they were certain He was in the tomb, but they were uncertain that they could keep Him there. A queer mixture of belief and unbelief! They had nothing more to fear but they would take no chances; they had rid themselves of His Presence but they feared He might walk again; He was dead and yet He might live.

This queer admixture of scepticism and faith accounts for the unbelievably appalling sight of soldiers drawn up in battle array against the dead, and a stone rolled in the face of one as lifeless as a stone. It is not ridiculous; it is not even humorous; it is the serious proof that when men revolt against Divinity, they must have the uncomfortable feeling that somehow God may yet be in the world. They will always be sure they have killed Christ, and yet they will guard His grave. As they celebrate their overwhelming victory they still have their eyes on their enemies; as they march to their wedding, they will hear the distant strains of their funeral march. *When God is the enemy, men can never be sure they have won the day.*

Their fears were justified. He rose as He said He would. But how? By the sounding of trumpets? By the tread of unseen footsteps sneaking past a Roman guard? No! In the point of darkest shade and deepest silence which just precedes the first full flush of day—out of the black air there suddenly blazed upon them a shape, "for an angel of the Lord came down from heaven, and coming up to the stone, rolled it away and sat upon it. His appearance was like lightning and his clothing was as white as snow; and for fear of him, those who were on guard were struck with terror and became as dead men." They would have been dauntless amidst the shock of battle and the din of arms, but they are dumb before a being who is not flesh and blood. Then turning to the women who stood his sight better than brave soldiers, the angel said: "Don't be afraid. I know that you are looking for Jesus Who was crucified. He is not here; He is risen, just as He said. Come see the place where He lay." "And, behold, Jesus met up with the women and said, 'Hail!' They came forward, took hold of His feet, and worshiped Him." *When God is the enemy, men can never be sure they have won the day!*

This lesson is as vital now as it was on the first Easter. Consider, for example, him who later on became St. Paul. Here was a son of Abraham, skilled in Greek dialectics, master of the Scriptures, prize student of the great Gamaliel of the Temple, who had heard about the new religion which a few Galilean peasants were beginning to preach not only throughout Israel, but throughout the Roman Empire. To Saul, it was only a flash in the pan; Christ was only an impostor; His followers were enemies of His own people and a scandal to the Greeks. Only a little pressure here and there and the dangerous sect would be exterminated. His first act was to assist at the martyrdom of Christianity's most brilliant deacon, Stephen. Saul then began a reign of terror, sitting at the very trials by which Christians were imprisoned, tortured, and put to death. Only one more bold stroke and Christianity would die. Armed with letters from Theophilus, the High Priest from Jerusalem, Paul got leave to open an inquisitorial court in Damascus. Christ the impostor was dead! Now Christianity the imposition would die! Pressing on over interminable stretches of desert plains east of Hermon, as the horses' hoofs clattered on the Roman pavement, suddenly with a fearsome terrified swerve, they were stopped by a blinding glare. A crash of a stampede, a babel of voices, then silence as the party saw the leader stretched on the ground. They heard him ask a question: "Who are you, Lord?"—and Paul, now stone blind heard the answer: "I am Jesus of Nazareth, Whom you are persecuting." He had seen the risen Christ; he was persecuting the living Christ in His Christians. Paul, who thought he had slain the foe, had lost the day. He was sure Christ was dead and yet he feared He might still be alive! He was alive and speaking to him. *When God is the enemy, men can never be sure they have won the day.*

Consider Russia. Here is a land covering one sixth of the earth's surface which, for the first time in the modern world, built up a definitely anti-God government. Seventy-two thousand churches and chapels were either closed, destroyed, or converted to secular uses; two hundred and fifty thousand clergy of all denominations were exiled or massacred, while millions of faithful were sent into exile for no other crime than because they believed in God. Education did not become godless as it largely is in America; it became anti-God; newspapers did not ignore religion, they attacked it, one sheet reaching a weekly circulation of seven million copies. Religion, it was said, was the opium capitalists fed to workers, and once capitalism was banished, religion would disappear into thin air.

They had killed Christ. He would never rise again. They could point out the grave. But were they satisfied? No! The anti-God forces asked the government for a guard; they asked that the frontier be sealed so that religion could never enter. They "sealed the tomb."

But why were they fearful? Why did they teach anti-God to children ten years of age who had never come under any religious influence? Why did they preach godlessness to the godless? Why did they attack religion in a land where no man or woman under twenty-seven could remember ever having heard the word God except in hate and derision? Russia did not believe in ghosts anymore than in God. If God were no more than a mental fancy or a ghost, why did they have to battle against belief in ghosts? It is because when people fight against God they are not fighting against a figment of the imagination; they are fighting against something as real as the thrust of a sword or an embrace. They do it for the same reason the Pharisees asked for soldiers to guard the tomb of Christ. Because man, even at the very moment he is most certain he has driven God off the face of the earth, really doubts his own victory. He disbelieves his own unbelief; he has no faith in his atheism; he doubts his own scepticism.

Ever since Good Friday man must always be fearful that closed doors cannot keep out the Light of the World. The doors of Russia were closed if ever doors of a nation have been closed to God, and yet somehow or other religion there did not die. Preachers of the Word of God—Jewish rabbis, Protestant ministers, Catholic priests—seem to have risen out of their graves. Despite all their past efforts at vigilance, wandering preachers are going about baptizing and teaching, performing religious marriages, soldiers are wearing crosses as the lesson of Easter rings out again: "and the doors being shut [Jesus] stood in their midst and said, 'Peace be to you.'" *When God is the enemy, men can never be sure they have won the day.*

In Germany, one witnessed identically the same phenomenon. Its 'new' philosophers were convinced that the adoration of the race had supplanted the adoration of God. Through force of arms it closed all religious schools in Bavaria, suppressed the Catholic press, and exiled and imprisoned Christian ministers. The race was set up as a counter-Church, as propaganda and secret service and faked trials imposed the false ideology of German blood as the Incarnation of a German myth.

The German Government was sure it had killed Christ and He would never rise again. And yet in the same breath it, too, set a guard over the tomb of Christianity. Why if redemption is dead and race is alive, did they go out of their way to persecute a dead thing? Why did the enemies of the Church go to Germany's Pilate and say: "Give us a guard—The dead thing may rise again"? They did it only because *when God is the enemy, men can never be sure they have won the day!*

What is true of nations is true of conscience. The millions of men in our land whose lives are not right with God and who because their deeds are evil court atheism; who sin with impunity and call forth superstition; who are convinced that religion is dying because it is only "the opium of the people"— these are the very men who as they awake at night, live in a terrible, awful dread of dying. They are sure there is no God behind conscience, but they send the soldiers of excitement, hurry, and noise to drown out its call. They have buried religion, but religion will not bury them. They leave Christ alone, but Christ will not leave them alone. Why? Because *when God is the enemy, man can never be sure he has won the day!*

Now turn the Easter lesson around: When man has lost the day, God comes back to save him. Man lost the day in Eden when he succumbed to the snares of Satan, and God promised a Redeemer to save him from sin. Man lost the day on Good Friday when he nailed the only true Goodness this earth has ever seen to an ignominious tree, and God returned on Easter day to save him from his own deceits. It is a peculiar fact of history that man never seems so much to need God as when his own strength has failed him; God does most for us when, like Peter, we have labored all night long and taken nothing.

We are at such a phase in modern history in this hour. Man has definitely lost the day. All the things in which he trusted—democracy, education, economics, science, and humanism—have failed him. Education, broken loose from religion, trains the mind to dying facts and useless theories to the utter neglect of the will, and in the end begets only a group that can rationalize evil. Science has ceased to deal with realities by becoming pseudo-mystical while armament builders have used its findings for the destruction of human life. Philosophy lost its mind, then its soul, and became only a history of theories, sure of only one of them, namely, that we can not know. Economics, making profit instead of man the purpose of production, devours its surplus for the sake of keeping prices up. Nineteenth-century democracy became a reactionary liberalism so divorced from truth that freedom has become synonymous with license.

Man has lost the day! The arms in which he has trusted have failed; the staff on which he has leaned has broken. Our cures were only deferred executions. Each idol man has built has collapsed in its turn; each Babel has confused his speech and is a great brotherhood of woe. But all is not hopeless. When man has lost the day, God comes back to save him. The Church which has been in exile for four hundred years during the days when individualism ran riot and reacted in collectivism, is now like the risen Christ coming back on a mission of rescue. She is moving against the frontiers of a cracking civilization. Man is just beginning to realize he crucified that which alone could save him. Like the prodigal son he discovered there was no place like the Father's house. We are at the beginning of a great spiritual renaissance in the world. The Church in the next generation will be filled not only with those who have been born into it, but also with those who have been re-born into it. The communion rail will be peopled not only by those who like John stood at a cross and an empty tomb, but those who like the centurion pierced the side of Christ there to find love revealed. The most adventurous leaders in modern society, those who feel a burning indignation at the frightful ravages of a godless world, are confessing by their confusion that there is no other place to go than back to what they thought was a tomb but what in reality is an empty grave. Ask them why they seek God now when they are so sure humanism has failed and they will say: "Because we live in a social world in which men are bound together corporately into nations, groups, and international society. I therefore do not want an individual religion or an individual philosophy anymore than I want an individual astronomy or an individual multiplication table. I want to feel my dependence on God corporately, to pray socially, and to offer a corporate sacrifice to the living God. That I find in the Church of one faith, one Lord, one Baptism, because it is infused by the Pentecostal soul which makes all one with the spirit of the living Christ." Others will say: "I want a messenger who does not tamper with the message. This I find in the Church which, as the messenger of the risen Christ, has refused to change the message to suit the fad and fancy of every individual to whom it is delivered."

But whatever be the reason, the fact is that the world is gradually beginning to see that our struggle is not between Democracy and Totalitarianism, or Socialism and Capitalism, but that it is between comradeship in anti-Christ and brotherhood in Christ that it must choose. And Easter reminds us that however bitter be the struggle we need have no doubts about the victory—for *when God is the ally, man can be sure he has won the day.*

Even as he turns from what he thought was a grave there stands beside him the Captain of Wars, not with wounds but with scars, the symbols of victory over death and hate, the spangled banner of the conqueror of evil. And when men have lost the day God comes back—back to His bleak earth with crosses silhouetted against a sky, bidding men reach out their hands and like other Thomases touch these adornings of victory to be cured of their unbelief. Live in hope for Christ is risen! Prepare for the new advent of the love of Christ! Bring your hearts to finish your salvation for the great tempests of Redemption are sweeping on! Say unto that risen Life!

> Bread of Thy Body give me for Thy fighting
> Give me to drink Thy Sacred Blood for wine
> While there are wrongs that need me for Thy fighting
> While there is warfare splendid and Divine.
> (*Studdert Kenedy*)

Bring your lesser calvaries to His great Calvary, for the *via crucis* is the *via pacis*. The way to peace is the cross. "Take up your cross and follow Me." Then under the muffled thunder of battle there shall ring out the cry of victory to the King of Kings and the Lord of Lords, *for when man has lost the day, God comes back to give him victory!*